COUPLES GROWING

COUPLES GROWING

A Companions' Guide to Long-distance Marriage

TONY GOUGH

DARTON, LONGMAN AND TODD
London

First published in 1991 by
Darton, Longman and Todd Ltd
89 Lillie Road, London SW6 1UD

British Library Cataloguing in Publication Data
Gough, Tony
Couples growing: a companions' guide to the long-distance marriage.
1. Married persons: Interpersonal relationships
I. Title
306.872

ISBN 0-232-51873-4

Phototypeset by Input Typesetting Ltd, London SW19 8DR
Printed and bound in Great Britain by
Courier International Ltd, Tiptree, Essex

For Jan,
my wife, companion, friend, lover,
and partner in our joyful growth together.
In loving gratitude for, and in celebration of,
our journey into life.

Contents

Acknowledgements

In preparation for this book I contacted a large number of people who are involved in the marriage enrichment scene. I am grateful to all those who replied and who sent their material to me. Appendix B contains the names and addresses of those from whom further details can be obtained.

I gratefully acknowledge the permission given by Dr Howard Clinebell, of the School of Theology at Claremont, California, to use the 'Marital Intimacy Check-up' from *The Intimate Marriage* (Howard J. Clinebell and Charlotte H. Clinebell, Harper & Row, 1970). It was good to make his acquaintance in Oxford many years ago and to learn from his wealth of wisdom and experience.

The 'Love-life Satisfaction Questionnaire' in chapter 12 owes much to the ideas suggested by Herbert A. Otto in *More Joy in Your Marriage* (Hawthorne, New York, 1969) and adapted by Larry Hof and William R. Miller in their *Marriage Enrichment: Philosophy, Process and Program* (Robert J. Brady Co., 1981). I gladly acknowledge my indebtedness to Herbert Otto for the original ideas and to Simon & Schuster (publishers) for permission to use it based on the modifications by Hof and Miller. The present form of the questionnaire is a completely revised and modified version of the original.

In compiling the 'Marital Role Expectations' exercise in chapter 9 I have freely adapted the ideas suggested by Larry Hof and William R. Miller's, *Marriage Enrichment*, which they found in N. Hurvitz's *Marital Roles Inventory Manual*

(Western Psychological Services, 1961). The version here is my own.

The poem *The Ache of Marriage* is taken from *O Taste and See* by Denise Levertov, copyright © 1964 by Denise Levertov Goodman. It is reprinted by permission of New Directions Publishing Corporation. The extract from *Come Love with Me and Be My Life and Surviving* by Peter McWilliams, copyright © 1967 and 1971, is reprinted by permission of Leo Press, 5806 Elizabeth Court, Allen Park, MI48101.

Special thanks to my friend Sue Wood (sometime manager of the Birmingham RELATE) for reading the chapters on intimacy. I especially valued her affirmation, enthusiasm and helpful comments on the original typescript and for her continuing encouragement. I also thank my friend Catherine Byron for pointing me in the direction of *The Bloodaxe Book of Contemporary Women Poets*, edited by Jeni Couzyn (Bloodaxe Books 1985). I am also grateful to the following for their help in my research: Benita Dyal and Christopher Vincent of the Tavistock Institute of Marital Studies, and the library staff of the Universities of Leicester and Nottingham.

I would also like to acknowledge thanks to all the other writers whose works are quoted liberally throughout this book. I hope you will be encouraged by these quotations to read their books in their entirety, in particular M. Scott Peck's *The Road Less Travelled*, Erich Fromm's *The Art of Loving*, Sam Keen's *To a Dancing God* and *The Passionate Life*, Tom Oden's *Game Free*, Harville Hendrix's *Getting the Love You Want*, Madonna Kolbenschlag's *Kiss Sleeping Beauty Goodbye*, Nena and George O'Neill's *Open Marriage*.

Special, mega-thanks to Willy Russell for his unforgettable play and film, *Shirley Valentine*. Only time will tell the significance of this film to the current debate on marriage growth and enrichment. And, not least, it's a smashing laugh!

September 1990 TONY GOUGH

Introduction

In spite of all the evidence to the contrary, the idea persists in our society that a way to instant happiness is to get married. That this idea is baseless, in terms of experience and statistics, does nothing to prevent its almost perverse persistence. Lemming-like, 94 per cent of us get married at least once.

Why is this so? Certainly, old Mother Nature has a part to play in this crazy scenario, for without offspring where would she be? But there is more to this phenomenon than mere biology. The influence of sociology and psychology also play an important part in this seemingly fatal attraction. The biblical dictum, 'It is not good for the man to be alone', seems to hang like a divine magnet over the whole of humankind, drawing the sexes together.

Amazingly, there is still much magical thinking attached to the idea of marriage. Hollywood has much to answer for, not least in its function as 'the factory of dreams'. Yet Hollywood only represented a projection of our mythical dreams of happiness on to a larger screen than our minds. Most of the idyllic 'happy endings' were not invented by the film industry. Fairy stories have played a large part in shaping the minds and expectations of generations. Magical thinking is far from dead, and many of us live out the expectation that it is marriage that will bring us the desired goal of everlasting bliss. The reality appears to be that a lot of frogs have to be kissed before we find our prince or princess. Even then, as likely as not, they may turn out to be far from ideal.

So we're now being forced out of the luxury of celluloid dreams.

The last decades of the twentieth century are witnessing dramatic changes in our traditional attitudes towards marriage. Fewer people are getting legally married; while 15.4 people in every thousand married in 1938, by 1983 this proportion had fallen to 13.9.[1] The new breed of 'living as married' is on the increase, as is the divorce rate, now running at 40 per cent of all marriages. A lower proportion of divorced people are remarrying. The libertarian voices that clamoured for easy sex now have to recognize the risk of AIDS, and campaigns for easier divorce have had some unforeseen social consequences. As the 'death of the family' comes into prospect, some radicals welcome this, but many other people are turning their attention away from *mending* marriages (the counselling process) to the *maintenance* of basically sound marriages. This is not a matter of having to choose one or the other; we need both the marriage 'paramedics' with their counselling skills at the bottom of the cliff for those who fall through the matrimonial fence and come to grief, as well as the 'maintenance fitters' who are attempting to keep the safety fence intact at the top of the cliff. The emphasis is now turning towards prevention rather than cure.

Hence this book. It attempts to answer the question, 'How can I keep my basically sound and satisfying marriage healthy?' The answer lies in the key word 'growth'. Like all living things, human relationships can grow and be fruitful, or they can wither and die.

I begin, therefore, in Part 1, with a brief look at the contemporary trends in our British society, recognizing that they are changing at an increasingly rapid pace even as I write. In Part 2, I look at some of the familiar obstacles to the process of growth in marriages and how we can understand and rectify them. Part 3 outlines the principles of the modern marriage enrichment movement, now espoused widely by both secular and religious organizations. Part 4 is the major part of the book, in which I outline how a marriage can be enriched in the important areas of intimacy, especially sexual intimacy. There are self-help exercises offered as a means of earthing the principles in actual practice. Chapter 13 gives one couple's experience of attending a marriage enrichment weekend and the effects it could have upon the average marriage. The Postscript is a moving account of Charles Rassieur's communication to his wife which illustrates beautifully the notion of marriage not as a life-sentence but as a day-by-day choice of the other person as companion and lover. In Appendix A, I have added a special note for those who are in their second or subsequent marriage, because there are special factors that need to be taken into consideration, not least the 'ghosts' of their former relationships. Appendix B contains some addresses of organizations from whom further details of the marriage enrichment movement can be obtained.

Woody Allen says in his film, *Annie Hall*: 'Relationships are like sharks. They keep moving forward or they die.' Without pushing the metaphor too far, we can recognize the truth that marriages that are not 'moving forward' are in danger of extinction. I offer this book in the hope that many marriages will be able to move out of their stuck and often unrewarding experiences into the full potential of human happiness and joy that is waiting to be discovered.

PART 1

Marriage Today: Contemporary Trends

Sir, it is so far from being natural for a man and a woman to live in a state of marriage, that we find all the motives that they have for remaining in that connection, and the restraints which civilised society imposes to prevent separation, hardly sufficient to keep them together.

Samuel Johnson

1. Marriage: An Ailing Institution and Harbinger of Destruction?

Dr Johnson's eighteenth-century strictures have an uncanny ring about them as we consider the future of the institution of marriage at the end of the twentieth-century. Many are questioning its prospects of survival in the twenty-first.

Marriage has become such a common part of our accepted way of life that anyone standing up and arguing against it might seem to be voting against motherhood and apple-pie. It would certainly be regarded as a direct attack against the 'British Establishment' – everything that we consider secure, desirable and part of a way of life that most of us have thought of as unassailable. To be anti-marriage would be tantamount to being anti-British.

An ailing institution?

However, there are some who, in all seriousness, challenge the desirability and even the 'healthiness' of marriage, the very basis of family life as we have known it for at least the past two thousand years. Are such people to be written off as cranks or – worse – feminist militants? To do so would be too simplistic for words. Many voices are being heard which claim marriage to be an obsolete institution that began in the world of sexual politics. Sam Keen offers an interesting insight:

> Radical feminists claim that men, being physically

> stronger than women, formed a conspiracy and invented marriage as a way of capturing the exclusive sexual rights to a female and enslaving women. According to the sort of man who reads *Playboy*, women invented marriage as a way to contain the wandering affections of the naturally promiscuous male and to ensure that they would have somebody to bring home the bacon and protect their young. Both explanations demean marriage and the intelligence of men and women.[2]

Other voices draw attention to the unhappiness and misery to be found in countless marriages today. Denise Levertov in her poem 'The Ache of Marriage' describes the experience of many people:

> The ache of marriage:
>
> thigh and tongue, beloved,
> are heavy with it,
> it throbs in the teeth
>
> We look for communion
> and are turned away, beloved,
> each and each
>
> It is leviathan and we
> in its belly
> looking for joy, some joy
> not to be known outside it
>
> two by two in the ark of
> the ache of it.

Marriage can indeed become a kind of Noah's Ark, a means of survival only for those who are prepared to forego their independence and even their individual identity. As institutions of all kinds come under the microscope of social investigation – which they must inevitably do in order to retain any vestige of contemporary relevance – the institution of marriage cannot claim special immunity to such a process.

The Noah's Ark syndrome often means that marriage can become a prison, a means of denying one's own unique personhood.

Harbinger of destruction?

The late Dr David Cooper, writing in 1971, regarded the traditional understanding of 'the family', which is the outcrop of marriage, as a questionable asset. He mentioned four factors which operate within the family 'often with lethal but always with stultifying consequences':

1. The glueing together of people based on each person's sense of incompleteness.
2. The formation of roles for the family members rather than the creation of the conditions for a free assumption of identity.
3. The family in its function as primary socializer of the child instils social controls in its children that tend to recreate the parents' own family model and works towards, not the survival of the child in society, but its submission to it.
4. The family instils into its children a system of taboos which is achieved by the implantation of guilt, 'the sword of Damocles that will descend on the head of anyone who prefers their own choices to those enjoined on them by the family and the wider society'.[3]

Since marriage stands as the basis on which the traditional family is constructed, it is not difficult to see that David Cooper's broadside had the institution of marriage clearly within his sights. Needless to say, the institution has survived. But for how long?

In 1973, Khoren Arisian reflected some of these criticisms of modern marriage in his helpful book, *The New Wedding*, where he wrote:

> We are in the midst of a pervasive and passionate

> criticism, in some cases a revulsion, against marriage as a kind of death trap for individual self-development. One recalls Colette's haunting, perceptive comments on how the institution of marriage has over the ages relentlessly inflicted its 'small deaths' on both men and women.[4]

There is nothing startlingly new in such analyses of family life. We have only to recall the ancient stories and myths, such as that of Oedipus and his family, to recognize that families have traditionally been the focus of horrendous violence, pain and conflict. As in the case of Oedipus, not every outcome could be satisfactorily described as '*small* deaths'! Leo Tolstoy, reflecting Russian life in the 1860s, wrote in the opening words of *Anna Karenina*, 'All happy families are more or less like one another; every unhappy family is unhappy in its own particular way.'

However, Madonna Kolbenschlag, in her book *Kiss Sleeping Beauty Good-Bye*, challenges Tolstoy's statement:

> Today, an inversion of Tolstoy's maxim might be a more accurate reflection of the contemporary scene. It is, in fact, in the 'typical' families, the ones most closely modelled on the 'norm', where unhappiness is rampant. This suggests that the problems allied to marriage and family in this era are not problems of deviance from the norm, but of adherence to it. The stresses, the breakdowns, have a structural rather than personal origin. But we resist admitting that there may be something wrong with the fundamental structure of marriage and family.[5]

Some social commentators are therefore seeing marriage as the Big Bad Wolf, the harbinger of all that is stifling of human growth and self-development. Wedlock can become deadlock! As we have noted briefly above, there is ample evidence, once we turn over the marital stone, that all kinds of unhealthy things can come crawling out from underneath.

The sheer weight of unhappiness that thousands of people suffer year in and year out – only partly reflected in our divorce rates (for many do not avail themselves of that particular exit) – is too great for us to ignore. Even *The Times*, that bastion of the establishment and respectability, and hardly a hot-bed of radicalism, could proclaim:

> If marriage were a motor car, it would have been banned by now. Its safety record is appalling – 170,000 breakdowns annually according to one marriage expert, with a yearly 'repair' bill to the nation of £2 billion. Most of us spend a great deal of energy trying to keep it on the road but what are its chances past the year 2000?[6]

To begin with, it seems that there are fewer people buying this particular form of transport. According to the *OPCS Monitor: General Household Survey* for 1988,[7] more couples are living together unmarried than ever before. This is also evidenced by the rise in births outside of marriage, now running at around 26 per cent of all live births. At the same time, the UK has the highest rate of marriage per head of the population than any other country in the European community. However, there does seem to be a change of attitude towards marriage which lies behind some of the more recent statistics.

2. The Changing Pattern of Marriage

First, and by far the most influential agents of change, there are the changing attitudes in our society towards gender issues – the way men and women regard and relate to one another. Bastions of male chauvinism still survive, of course, but the women's movement is continuing to have a radical effect upon the attitudes most of us inherited from our past. Women are less and less thought of as 'housekeepers'; indeed, many women earn more than their husbands and this can become a source of friction in their marriage. Men are also less and less regarded as a 'free meal ticket'. Partnership is now replacing the previous emphasis on 'possession'. The old male-dominated contract is becoming a thing of the past. Joint bank accounts and ownership in the marital home are now commonplace.

Secondly, due to the estimated shortage of school-leavers in the 1990s, more positions are becoming available to married women than ever before. Careers and job satisfaction are therefore opening up to women who hitherto may have seen marriage as their only base for a secure future. Many women living with men in stable relationships outside marriage would be included in this category. The figures show that by the year 2000, women will account for 44 per cent of the nation's workforce. In the USA the proportion is over 50 per cent.

Thirdly, the message of the 'appalling safety record' of marriage is thoroughly understood by most people. According to the Office of Population Censuses and Surveys

(OPCS) the number of women aged 18–49 cohabiting with their man-friends almost tripled between 1979 and 1988: 3 per cent in 1979, 6 per cent in 1987 and 8 per cent in 1988. The survey also shows that 'one of the most notable features' of this period since the Second World War (1945) is the increase in the number of people living alone. More than a quarter of all households now consist of just one person.[8]

Fourthly, cohabitation by divorcees is rising. Of divorced women, for example, 28 per cent of the 18–49 age-group were cohabiting.

Fifthly, in a recent Gallup Poll (June 1990)[9] it was shown that 82 per cent of people living as married, and 61 per cent of married couples, thought that the trend *away* from the traditional marriage (with the man supporting the family and the wife staying at home) was a good thing.

Even such a brief glance at our national statistics confirms what most of us are aware of from our own family and social contacts: that more people are seeking an alternative to the traditional marriage, fewer divorced people are seeking remarriage, more people are prepared to live alone. Where does this leave the institution of marriage?

The future of marriage

It is interesting to examine some of the ideas previously held about marriage in order to appreciate how the current changes are affecting the institution of marriage. For example, Christopher Clulow, of the Institute of Marital Studies, says,

> For some people getting married is an end in itself. With marriage comes a socially-conferred role and status . . . marriage is viewed as a social institution and expected to provide ready-made answers to some of the most important questions in life: 'Who am I?' 'How should I behave?' 'Where do I find my niche in the community?'[10]

For women, though rarely for men, the old tradition was

that their role and status were gained from the relationship to their spouse. Married women were introduced as 'Mr Brown's wife', 'the doctor's wife' or merely as 'the wife'. Few women are prepared to allow that to happen today. Women – and these changes particularly affect them – now want to be identified as people in their own right and their existence is felt to depend less on their marital status and relationship to their husband and more, as Anne Dickson affirms in her book title, *A Woman in Your Own Right.*[11]

The question is now being actively addressed: Is there a future for marriage? Since around 94 per cent of people try marriage at least once, its future would appear secure. But its meaning and purpose have undergone dramatic changes in recent years, not least in the separation of the two distinct roles of 'husband-and-wife' from 'mother-and-father'. Sociologically (and theologically, in the churches' reforms of their marriage ceremonies) the procreation of children is no longer the prime purpose of marriage.

Marriage as companionship

These factors are leading many people today to recognize that the institution of marriage is not so secure as some would like to think. Promises set in concrete are far from the minds of most couples getting married today. A more dynamic (and healthy) view of marriage is emerging, and this is focused on the notion of marriage as companionship.

In 1927 a book was published by Judge Ben B. Lindsey entitled *The Companionate Marriage* in which he put forward the suggestion that men and women could marry solely for the purpose of enjoying companionship and sex without producing children. It is not hard to guess the response to that full-frontal assault on post-Victorian society. Few today would react unfavourably to such a description of modern marriage. It is significant in this context to notice the radical shift of emphasis in the modern marriage service of the Church of England, produced in 1980. The service produced in 1662 included the words, 'First, (marriage) was ordained for the procreation of children . . .' Compare that to the 1980 service which says, 'Marriage is given, that husband and wife may comfort and help each other . . . It is given, that with delight and tenderness they may know each other in love, and, through the joy of their bodily union, may strengthen the union of their hearts and lives.' In other words, the procreation of children is no longer believed to be the prime reason for getting married. (One clergyman I know refuses to use the old 1662 service if the couple practise any form of contraception since this seems at odds with the purpose of marriage in the old Book of Common Prayer.)

In our modern climate, at least two major changes are affecting marriage today. First, more and more couples are choosing either to have no children at all or to delay having them until the woman is in her mid-thirties. Career and financial interests chiefly govern the first choice, and influence the second. Secondly, with the advent of easier divorce, couples who find themselves locked into an unworkable and unsatisfying marriage can end it. The latest divorce statistics suggest that four in ten couples make this choice.[12] Betty Yorburg writes:

> In family life, the formerly dominant values of loyalty, obligation, deference and self-sacrifice are slowly being displaced by the standards of happiness, companionship, erotic gratification for both sexes, equalitarianism and compatibility, at least among the upper strata in advanced industrial societies.[13]

Whether we like it or not, many of the old 'oughts' and 'shoulds' of marriage are breaking down, and new values are coming into focus. Becoming parents is now a separate issue from becoming partners for many people marrying today.

While the 'new marriage' still includes a strong sense of commitment, nowadays the traditional promise of 'till death us do part', is considered not so much a morally binding statement as a declaration of intent. The word 'death' itself is interpreted more widely than the physical death of a partner. It is capable of application to the relationship as a whole, to the death of love and meaning within it. One shorthand term for this focus is 'the open marriage' (see further, pp. 41–2).

Open *v*. closed marriages

For some, the idea of an open marriage has about it the whiff of promiscuity. 'Open' is thought to be the equivalent of 'loose'! While the concept of an 'open' marriage is certainly flexible by definition, it is not in contrast to 'moral'. Its distinctiveness lies in its contrast to the 'closed' type of marriage, the inflexible, stifling, possessive, glued-together, 'Noah's Ark' kind of relationship which usually ends up being far too claustrophobic for comfort. While there has been no 'National Campaign for the Liberation of Marriage', new ideas concerning marriage have been filtering down to the grass-roots in the slow way that social reforms usually develop. Choices gradually become viable that may never have been considered before.

There are thousands of couples today living a variant of the 'open' marriage although they may not be conscious of the fact. They have not become fully-paid up members of the 'NCLM'; far more importantly, they have begun to respond to their own inner needs concerning the kind of relationship they want. People are becoming aware of new kinds of 'coupling' models on offer, and the 'ball-and-chain' model is now virtually extinct, an exhibit in the National Marital History Museum. Fewer and fewer marriages are based on the predictable models of the past. More and more couples are writing, or rewriting, their own marriage contract to accommodate their contemporary needs for love and happiness, rather than use the old 'off-the-peg', 'take-it-or-leave it', 'you-belong-to-me' models of marriage that have proved so damaging in the past.

> The open marriage, in contrast, encourages growth for both husband and wife. Therefore their union thrives on change and new experiences. With change, new constellations of behaviour, new ways of relating, new knowledge of the self, and an increased dynamism of interaction between the two become possible. Even falling in love with the other can become a cyclically recurring event. As each becomes more attractive to the other by means of their individual growth and their developing knowledge of one another, their union grows in strength, constantly revitalized, constantly expanding.[14]

I have included as a Postscript to this book the moving letter by Charles Rassieur to his wife, Ginni, in which he gives his personal reasons for continuing to choose her as his wife and companion.

The new marriage

The attitude that regarded a marriage certificate as either free meals, or a free housekeeper, for life is now on the way out. Few marriages were ever consciously considered in these hard-headed, business-like terms, but that view has prevailed unconsciously for decades. Partnership is now replacing the previous emphasis on 'possession'. The old male-dominated contract is fast becoming a thing of the past, especially where ownership of property and other assets is concerned. These phenomena are perhaps the symbols of a new approach to modern marriage. They are becoming less and less matters of debate and decision; for many younger people they are simply the right way to go about laying the foundation of their relationship. More to the point in this present discussion, more couples are coming into a new understanding of how good marriages work. They are not prepared to accept unthinkingly the ancient 'wedlock-deadlock' syndrome. Marriages are not now seen as set in concrete, or existing solely through pieces of legal paper. The new marriage is flexible, equal, open, negotiable, capable of change. Above all, it is open to growth and development.

Growth implies life. It means a full recognition that relationships can live and grow; but they can also fail to thrive, and die. There are no guarantees.

No guarantees – since there are many factors that determine the outcome of a marriage. These are as diverse and complicated as the two people who comprise the union. Their attitudes towards, as well as their personal histories of, sharing, giving, receiving, self-esteem and of dependency will all influence its outcome. Love is often conceived in terms of dependency, as M. Scott Peck writes,

> When you require another individual for your survival, you are a parasite on that individual. There is no choice, no freedom involved in your relationship. It is a matter of necessity rather than love. Love is the free exercise of choice. Two people love each other only when they are quite capable of living without each other but *choose* to live with each other.[15]

There are plenty of existing marriages that are capable of renewal, and this hope and possibility lies at the heart of our journey towards a new marriage. It will not entail a return to what we once had – for that is illusion. It means finding fresh meaning, love and happiness in the relationship we are now in. It may involve a hard, long look at the way things are with each other just now, yet I believe it can be worthwhile. This book will focus on such issues.

Experience teaches us, however, that relationships that began as an ecstatic union can easily degenerate into a sharing of mutual misery. It is therefore important that at this point in our discussion we identify some of the hindrances we are likely to find in the growth of our marriage towards fulfilment and happiness. What are some of the rocks upon which our marriage can founder?

PART 2

Some Obstacles to Growth

3. Marriage: Growing or Dying?

Good relationships don't just happen. They're worked at.

We often find ourselves envying the relationship of some of our friends who seem to be in basic harmony with one another. They can occasionally disagree with each other, sometimes sharply, but underneath they still remain committed to their friendship and come out of their disagreements with their relationship not only intact, but even enriched through the process. Are these the marriages that are mysteriously made in heaven, and which no amount of aggravation can destroy? Do they possess some secret powers denied to us lesser mortals?

Our friends, of course, may be blissfully unaware that their relationship is radically different to that of other couples. Somehow or other they have discovered a constructive model of how a relationship grows. That may be the secret that we ourselves have still to discover.

Relationships, first and foremost, are not made with built-in, fail-safe mechanisms which prevent erosion and decay. However much in love we may be – and in spite of all the siren voices of our pop culture that invite us to believe that 'All you need is love' and that 'Love changes everything' – there is no guarantee that our love or our relationship will last. The issue seems to boil down to this: marriages that are not busy growing are busy dying.

On the other hand, we can all recall the breakdown of those marriages we would have thought of as fireproof. News of impending separation and divorce reaches us with a sense of shock. 'Bert and Bertha?' we say, 'who'd have believed that possible? They seemed so inseparable, so right for each other. What on earth could have happened?' (The concern hidden beneath such consternation is, of course, not so very hard to understand; for if solid marriages like that of Bert and Bertha are at risk, whose marriage can be thought of as safe?)

We need to be aware of that vital stage of a relationship which so often gets overlooked. After the *birth* of a relationship, there needs to come the *growth* in that relationship. This introduces us to the important concept that *relationships are dynamic, not static.* In other words, they don't just stand still. It took the Church some time to accept the ideas of Copernicus and others that the earth is not the centre of the universe and that the sun does not revolve around it. The earth moves! Similarly it takes some people by surprise to learn that their most important relationships do not stand still; they move and change and can deteriorate, and they can die. Marriages are dynamic relationships; they are in motion whether we like it or not. I am changing and so is my wife. The point is this: can our relationship withstand the changes going on in me and in her? Is our marriage going to be enriched by these changes, or threatened and destroyed by them?

It is very significant that this growing phase, the heart of the relationship, is the one that so often gets overlooked in terms of time, energy, and commitment. It is, of course, a natural development that, after the heady days of courtship, the relationship should develop in a less intense way; but that is a long way from the popular view that a relationship, once founded, is somehow mysteriously self-vitalizing and self-enervating.

This necessary growth in a relationship often gets overlooked, since it is not amenable to the kind of visual monitoring that a child's growth is. They have wall-charts and, each birthday, we take a new measurement to see how they have grown during the year. We have the year by year comparison through our photograph albums. Relationships have no such convenient 'wall-chart'. Were we to notice that our children are not gaining in the expected height and weight as they grow older, we would very quickly call in the medical experts to correct what was happening. If children fail to thrive, we are naturally concerned. We need to channel similar concern to relationships that fail to thrive.

The truth seems to be that those relationships that are not growing – in terms of love, trust, joy and the spontaneous celebration of their life together – are likely to decay. We all know of marriages where the couple's tomorrows are going to be, in a quite predictable way, a repetition of all their yesterdays. They are stale, boring, uneventful, lacking in joy and spontaneity, and nothing ever seems to change. Instead of maturing they just get older.

Shirley Valentine

Willy Russell's memorable play (and subsequent award-winning film) *Shirley Valentine*, addresses the dangers and the opportunities implicit in this kind of stale marital situation. Joe and Shirley Bradshaw have been married for about twenty years, and their children have left home. In the film, Shirley (now 42) says, 'Fancy a change? I do. I've reached the stage where I'm talking to the kitchen wall. In fact, I'll let you into a little secret – it's become my best friend.' Her views of marriage, as on the rest of life, are often hilarious, but always with a hint of sadness and longing behind them. 'Marriage', she says, 'is like the Middle East – no solution. You keep your head down, observe the curfew and hope the ceasefire holds.' And as for sex: 'Sex is like the supermarket,' says Shirley. 'Overrated. It's just a lot of pushin' and shovin' and you still come out with very little in the end!' Shirley begins to wonder to herself, in the song accompanying the film credits, whatever happened to 'The girl who used to be me', the young Liverpudlian girl, Shirley Valentine,.

This profoundly funny film has a very serious message wrapped up in its humour, and this has not been lost on the thousands of 'Shirley Valentines' in lifeless marriages. 'Shirley' has spoken for many bored and undervalued housewives who were prepared to take risks in order to change their circumstances for the better. Not that women have a monopoly on boredom. Men can also get stuck in unproductive ruts and find themselves caught in the traditional emptiness of mind-sapping vapidity. The only difference between a rut and a grave is the depth and – it's possible to get out of a rut!

4. Five Obstacles to Growth

Why is it that some marriages, like that of Shirley Valentine, lack the necessary growth in their development as the years pass by? Let us identify some of the unhealthy obstacles to growth in marriage, and illustrate their deadly effect.

1. Mistaken assumptions

The first obstacle, of course, is the failure to recognize the existence of a problem. Some of the assumptions we make about our marriage can be mistaken and, in the case of many married couples, hardly ever get checked out. Things are merely taken for granted. Here are a few assumptions you might like to check out with yourself. Do you or your partner hold any of these?

> 'My husband wouldn't think of leaving me.'
> 'Of course my wife is sexually fulfilled.'
> 'She couldn't live without me.'
> 'Our marriage was made in heaven.'
> 'He needs me.'
> 'She doesn't even know the meaning of an affair.'
> 'Of course he's happy – why do you ask?'
> 'We never argue – why should we?'
> 'Our marriage is as safe as houses.'
> 'We're OK. After all, we did promise "till death us do part", didn't we?'
> 'Divorces don't happen in our family.'

'Our marriage doesn't need any help – it's just fine.'
'Whoever would give my wife/husband a second look?'

We can almost hear the complacency oozing from some of these assumptions. The first step towards putting something right is to recognize that something is wrong. And assuming that marriages regenerate themselves by some automatic and mysterious process blinds us to the truth that they do not. Mistaken assumptions are usually discovered only after the collapse of the marriage, and the inevitable post-mortem is held. 'How could this happen to me?' someone asks. 'Everything seemed to be going so well!'

The antidote to mistaken assumptions is the process called 'checking out'. (There some useful 'checking out exercises' included on pp. 90–1 and 106–8.) Naturally you do not have to take the marital temperature every day; to do so would indicate some deeply rooted insecurity. The need for constant reassurance may be a sign of a character disorder rather than the process of 'checking out'. 'Are you happy, darling?' is at least an invitation to my wife to think about how she feels about our relationship. It also shows my concern for her happiness, and that it is just as important to me as it is to her. It is a 'door opening' exercise in which we can (if we allow ourselves to do so) express anything we feel unhappy about. 'Well, now that you ask . . .' could begin a profitable (if painful) exploration into some sources of pain or frustration. Such an invitation shows that I *care*. It can also prevent another block to the growth of our marriage.

2. Taking our partner for granted

This is, of course, closely related to an assumption but deserves specific mention because it features so regularly in marriage counselling.

Time and again, partners complain of being taken for granted. It is experienced as a lack of appreciation. Some men get so used to their meals being served on time, their shirts ironed, their beds made, that they can easily forget that their partner actually puts a lot of energy and time into making things run smoothly in the home. Some women can get so used to money appearing mysteriously in the bank account, the bills being paid, the car always at the ready, their credit card accounts settled regularly, that they, too, can forget that someone, somewhere, is putting resources and time into this side of their marriage. Of course, in our modern society where stereotyped gender roles are changing rapidly, not all these examples may apply to *your* marriage, but the point I am making is this: it is all too easy for us to take one another for granted, and for the nurturing expressions of appreciation to get lost in the day-to-day busyness of life. Sometimes we get so used to a lack of appreciation that the occasional gift of a bunch of flowers, box of chocolates or a cigar may be a signal for great anxiety on the part of the recipient. 'What have you been up to?' they may ask. 'Are you feeling guilty about something?' Perhaps the recent resurgence in the interest of St Valentine's Day (February 14) is one encouraging example that people are taking their partners less for granted than hitherto. But an annual token gesture is never enough; there are still too many marriages that are dying for lack of words of appreciation and encouragement.

Think for a moment of the things that your partner does for you on a day-to-day basis. They do not need thanking every day, for this would soon lose its impact, and become a meaningless ritual. Yet unappreciativeness can soon become the norm in a marriage, and we begin to take the other person for granted. We know how this feels when it happens to us. 'Oh, roses; my favourite. I'll just pop them in water!' is all very well, but we would like a 'thank you' with or without a kiss. Appreciation is like the vital vitamins our body needs for healthy functioning, and many marriages die for the lack of these emotional nutrients.

Taking certain things for granted in a relationship can, however, be an expression of trust. All good and growing relationships are based on trust in the other person. For example, some people simply take for granted that their partner will not deliberately inflict pain on them. They trust them sufficiently to believe that they have their best interests at heart. But taking an agreed basis of a relationship for granted is quite different from taking the *person* for granted. While we may assume that the principles on which our relationship is based are secure it does not follow that we should take our partner for granted in all the practical ways in which those principles find expression. I may 'take for granted' that there will be a meal waiting for me when I get home from work (unless my wife has said otherwise), but I need to express my appreciation for that meal on a regular basis. An appropriate 'taking for granted' applies to principles rather than to people, but even those may need the occasional revision and reaffirmation.

Just as a constant fussing over bodily health can be a sign of hypochondria, so an obsessive ferreting around in our marriages for some sign of disease can be equally unhealthy. Healthy bodies do not need constant check-ups, but an occasional health-check can prove a very useful precaution to take. So in our marriages. Although we take its general 'health' for granted, an occasional marriage review can be a useful precaution against the development of a hidden disease.

3. Dishonesty

This familiar block to the growth of a marriage represents the unwillingness (usually based on fear) to be totally honest with our partner. There can be no growth in a marriage without honesty; why, then, do we find honesty so hard to practise?

The usual excuse, of course, is that if we were to tell our partner 'the truth' it would upset them. Therefore, this justifies our being untruthful. I recall one woman who discovered a packet of contraceptives in her son's car. She was shocked, but defended her keeping this from her husband by her belief that 'it would destroy him'. As we proceeded to a deeper exploration of her feelings, it was in fact she who was being 'destroyed' by the discovery. She had never contemplated her only son as a sexual male; this brought about a crisis in her life. What prevented her from dealing with it at first was her fantasy that sharing the knowledge with her husband would destroy him. She was, in fact, protecting herself rather than her husband. Self-deception knows no bounds! We need to expose this popular 'reasoning' and see it as essentially unhealthy and self-protective.

Don't misunderstand me. I'm not saying it's a virtue to upset your partner deliberately, out of either malice or revenge. But it is all too easy to confuse the loving desire to protect our partner from hurt (for their benefit) with the desire to deceive our partner (for our own benefit). In most of the cases where one partner is holding out on the other because they don't want to upset them, the overriding motivation is that of self-interest and self-protection. In fact, it is the withholder who is gaining most from their imagined 'protection' of their partner.

Case Study: Peter and Pauline

This couple has been married for about eight years, and have one child. For several months, Peter has been having an affair with Alice, his next-door neighbour. Pauline is at present heavily pregnant with their second child, and although Peter considers himself to be happily married, he is unable or unwilling to give Alice up. To be honest with Pauline about her would upset her dreadfully, especially in her condition. So, Peter justifies his deception by withholding the truth from her.

Peter's self-justification is bogus. He is actually dreading the truth emerging about Alice. He would lose credibility with his wife, and with the rest of the family. Peter has a vested interest in not telling his wife about his affair. He justifies his deception of Pauline by saying that 'he wouldn't like to upset her.'

This is a typical example of the marital double-bind. Peter is 'damned if he does and damned if he doesn't' tell his wife. Yet in most cases, it is the ongoing deceit that can hurt more than the affair itself. When the offended spouse eventually discovers the truth, and begins to back-date the events, they can imagine their partner and their lover laughing at them behind their back. They feel that they have been made to look foolish. This is followed by a loss of self-esteem and confidence; it certainly entails a loss of trust in their spouse, whether temporarily or permanently time will tell. They resort to blaming themselves: 'I shouldn't have been so trusting/naive/blind,' they say. The affair is bad enough; but their partner's deceit often does by far the greater damage to their relationship and to their own self-esteem.

This is but one of many illustrations of how dishonesty can destroy a relationship. Holding out on pay rises, debt or the financial situation generally, is just as likely to provoke a crisis in the marriage when the truth emerges, as almost inevitably it will.

It really won't do to pretend that the truth is only withheld because it might upset the other partner. There are many things that, in the interests of the health of the marriage, need to be shared, but seldom are. It is a regular feature of marriage counselling to find someone pouring out to a total stranger all the hurt and pain inflicted by their partner, but which has never been shared with that partner. They feel frustrated, depressed, angry and helpless. But when they are invited to say how they feel to their *partner* there is a predictable response: 'Oh, I couldn't do that; he/she would get upset.'

It is still possible to be truthful *and* kind. Of course the truth often hurts. Expressing what you do not like in the marriage, disagreeing with your partner, saying 'yes' when you mean 'yes', instead of the usual 'no'; all of these can actually build the marriage up, not destroy it. Dishonesty is one of the most destructive obstacles to an ongoing and healthy marriage. Will Schutz says, 'Dishonesty holds me back, blocks me, stops my flow, ties up my energy, and exhausts me.'[16] And I believe he is right.

4. Self-denial

This is closely related to the dishonesty mentioned above. Again, it can look attractive, but it can be a wolf in sheep's clothing.

To be forever putting the other person first is popularly regarded as a virtue. (Indeed, much of the influence of Western Christendom has ingrained this idea in our social and cultural heritage.) Given our ability to bring evil out of good, we now use self-denial to deny our own needs and interests within our marriage. Such inappropriate denial of the self is common to many people. Of course, in a well-balanced marriage, we cannot have our own way all the time; neither, in our better moods, would we wish this. It is a sign of maturity when we can compromise with our partner in the interests of a fair distribution of the resources of the relationship. But the trouble is that some people submit totally to the needs and wishes of their partners, and get drained and worn-out in the process. They are the 'marriage martyrs', and their slogan is, 'Look what I've sacrificed for you . . . !'

Such self-denial is unhealthy, and more likely to result in the breakdown of the 'martyr' than in building up the marriage. Our human selves were not made to be denied; we need to be accepted, loved, celebrated. When we fail to accept and celebrate ourselves, we are offering to the marriage only a shell of ourselves. We then submit to the popular concept of a partner as 'our other half'. We are only half a person; they are (or represent) our 'other half'. It is a denial of the wholeness of our personality. A poem by Peter McWilliams is deeply relevant here:

I must conquer my loneliness
alone.
I must be happy with myself
or I have nothing
to offer you.
Two halves have little choice
but to join;
and yes, they do make a whole.
But two wholes
when they coincide . . .
that is beauty.
That is love.[17]

It is a major block to the growth of a relationship when partners constantly deny themselves and their own legitimate needs. I know how hard it is to change the habits of a lifetime, and to say directly what it is that we want either from the marriage or from our partner. This does not mean making impossible demands upon our partner or intimidating them. It means expressing our needs, our ideas, thoughts, wishes, hopes and fears in a direct rather than in an indirect way. It is to open the reality of ourselves to the reality of our partner. It often feels risky to do this, and we cannot always guarantee what the outcome will be. Yet without this exposure of our inner selves and our yearnings, hopes and dreams, we remain a stranger to our partner. George Eliot's words may help you discover the possibility of what a truly loving relationship can be like:

> Oh, the comfort, the inexpressible comfort, of feeling safe with a person; having neither to weigh thoughts nor measure words, but pour them all out, just as they are, chaff and grain together, knowing that a faithful hand will take and sift them, keep what is worth keeping, and then with a breath of kindness, blow the rest away.

How few of us know the security and joy of a relationship

based on these sentiments! And yet, they are within the reach of most of us.

5. The absence of 'prime time'

Lack of 'prime time' is one of the most damaging obstacles to the healthy growth of many marriages. The expression 'prime time' originated, I believe, in TV schedules and described those viewing hours when most people were watching their screens. It applied generally to the 7–10 p.m. slot, and of course the prized Television Audience Measurement ratings were related to the fees charged for the commercials during these hours.

The concept, therefore, is a useful one when applied to marriages. It refers to the need for couples to spend *quality* time together, not just at the end of the day when both partners are worn out: she (traditionally) by the children, and he (usually) by the hassles and tensions back at the office. Most marriages, I would dare say, run on this 'fag-end' offering of time to one another, when both individual and family resources are at their lowest. He has no time to listen to her hassles of the day, and she in turn has no inclination to listen to his pressures and stress at the office. They begin to get used to this 'blocking out' process, and gradually a tacit agreement is made that: 'I won't tell you my problems if you don't tell me yours.' Therefore, what is concerning each partner is deemed to be 'off limits', and only gets stored up with all the other hidden and unexpressed concerns. It becomes an unspoken agreement that he doesn't bring the office home with him, and that she doesn't bring up Timmy's fight with the neighbourhood kid. Both partners operate on a 'I-don't-want-to-know' basis, and immediately barriers are in place which can become impenetrable. They can affect other areas of the marriage too. Thoughts of 'Well, if she's not interested in my work, I'm not interested in hers' are nursed, and it is not long before resentment and hostility emerge against one another. A character in a poem by Jeni Couzyn is described thus:

> In her linen cupboard, newly ironed and neatly
> folded, she keeps her resentments like
> wedding presents – each week
> takes them out for counting not to
> lose any but would never think of
> using any being a lady.[18]

With so much that concerns the couple placed underneath the matrimonial carpet (or in the linen cupboard), what tends to happen is that a distancing soon becomes apparent. They begin to drift apart and to think, perhaps correctly, that the other partner does not care about them and their problems. Herein lies one of the major causes of matrimonial break-up. Nature abhors a vacuum. And if he/she won't listen, there's usually a nice person in the office or at the sports club who is very inviting and is eager to listen to my problems, and shows care and concern – 'not like my husband/wife'.

Giving time to one another, when we are fresh and open to the needs of our partner, is a prerequisite to a growing marriage. It is not so much a question of 'finding time' as 'making time', and this demands the reordering of our priorities. So often we get the marriage we deserve. Many married people spend more time on their hobbies than they do on their partner, giving as their excuse that they 'need a break' from family, work and home. While leisure activities are important, there are many things that couples can do together in terms of recreation and fun, including joining in gardening or cleaning the family car.

A year or two ago, my wife and I became painfully aware that our own time together was being severely eroded by business and family pressures. We made some conscious decisions focusing chiefly on our diary. Regular times were blocked off (weekends, anniversaries, 'red letter days', etc.), and there is no question that we have both felt the benefit from this conscious allocation of 'prime time' for one another. Some of those periods were spent in entertaining friends, visiting friends and relatives, walking, planning trips to local beauty spots, concerts – even jam-making together – and finding for ourselves a masseur! Prime time activities (or simply time when we do nothing but relax in one another's company) are deeply personal periods and you will have your own list of preferences once you give your mind to it. The absence of prime time is a fundamental cause of erosion in many marriages.

Removing this block to growth entails improving the amount of 'prime time' spent with one another, giving attention to one another, and listening at more than the casual level from behind the newspaper, or while watching TV.

Here are just five obstacles to the growth of a marriage relationship. It is no use there being life and vitality in a relationship if it is being continually frustrated by unhealthy blocks that prevent its flow. Mistaken assumptions, being taken for granted, dishonesty, self-denial and the absence of prime time spent with one another; these and other blocks all contribute to the slow deterioration of the marriage. A physical illustration is found in the presence of threatening proportions of cholesterol in our blood stream. Gradually, and silently, this clogs up the arteries, until the life force in the blood cannot pass through, and the person suffers a heart attack which can prove fatal. The medical profession is rightly drawing our attention to the need for regular check-ups, and to the dangers of letting blocked arteries reach life-threatening proportions. Is it not time that we applied the same principles to our marriages? Many of them 'die' because of these blocks, and the sad thing is that in the majority of cases it is entirely preventable. Marriages, too, can die of 'heart attacks' – the hearts broken by constant neglect and chronic lack of affirmation, which eventually give up in total despair and loss of hope.

Perhaps those of us who are married or living as married

could learn something from the warnings of the medical profession and apply similar preventive strategies to our relationships? It is to this 'preventive' aspect of the marriage relationship that the rest of this book is addressed. In practical terms, it means understanding the principles of good human relationships and finding an answer to the question, 'How can my partner and I improve our existing stable relationship?'

PART 3

The Principles of Marriage Enrichment

5. Modern Developments

The practice of 'marriage enrichment' began in the 1970s, and grew out of what came to be called the human potential movement.

> The social revolutions of the sixties gave way to the awareness explosion of the seventies . . . [It] began in several places, most prominently in a seemingly provincial, primarily [American] West Coast phenomenon known as the human potential movement. In the late 1960s, first California, then America, then the world, was introduced to a series of theories and techniques aimed at realizing the human potential.[19]

The main thrust of this movement was toward the fulfilment of all that human beings have within them to develop, and was all-inclusive: body, mind and spirit became the focus for fast-developing theories and therapies. In the 1990s, we are moving into the legacy of this movement with its passionate concern for the quality of human life and experience.

At about the same time as the human potential movement was developing, another major influence was gaining in popularity and momentum among women in the 1970s. This movement has been variously defined as the feminist movement and women's liberation, but is more generally described today as the women's movement.

Like most new movements in history, the women's movement had a long period of gestation. It arose from a growing awareness and recognition among women of their subservient place both in history and in modern society, and their desire to remedy this unjust situation. By the opening of the twentieth century there were women like Emmeline Pankhurst (1858–1928) who were drawing the attention of the public to the injustices of the absence of the franchise for women in Great Britain. The modern women's movement has never been a homogenous entity; nevertheless, there were several women who were pioneers in bringing greater awareness to the general public. Betty Friedan's book, *The Feminine Mystique*,[20] published in 1963, is believed by many to have signalled the beginning of the modern women's movement. Elaine Storkey writes, 'Her style was powerful and her many lectures very persuasive . . . One of the targets for her attack was Freudian psychology and the way it reinforced the traditional role of women whilst infusing them with guilt about their own inadequacies and failings as mothers.'[21] Among those who followed Betty Friedan, perhaps none made a bigger impact than Germaine Greer and her more popular book, *The Female Eunuch*.[22]

It was impossible that the institution of marriage should escape the fall-out from the public debate promoted by these two movements. Marriage is often seen as the very foundation of civilized society, and as marriages were seen to be more and more at risk, and divorce statistics were revealing the incredible failure rate, voices were being heard that heralded the 'end of civilization as we know it'. Occasionally, a strident 'feminist' voice would call for the wholesale destruction of the entire institution of marriage as the breeding ground of so much of the pain that women have experienced within it.

Surprisingly, as the institution of marriage came under the microscope it was found to be more healthy than had been previously thought. It may be sick, but it was not yet dead. Traditional weddings continue to have a popular appeal. Rather than any serious attempt to overthrow the institution of marriage, an initial reaction was to provide more resources for the programme of *mending* marriages. The kind of work undertaken by the National Marriage Guidance Council of Great Britain (now known as RELATE) is perhaps the most familiar. There is, however, the strange irony that while the Government spends around £3.5 million every day picking up the pieces after divorce, they give only around £1 million a year for marriage guidance and conciliation which may avert the divorce in the first place. These resources, however meagre, are of great benefit, but where does the basically healthy marriage fit into our national picture? This is where a second reaction is beginning to occupy a more central place in current thinking on marriage. There is now a national interest in the process of the *maintenance* of healthy marriages.

This shift of emphasis from mending to maintenance does not imply that a choice has to be made by the social services. Both are necessary. Marriage counselling (the mending process) and marriage enrichment (the maintenance process) represent the two sides of a healthy provision for those of us who have chosen marriage as a way of life. It also represents a shift away from the exclusive interest in pathology and the pain that ensues when marriages go wrong.

Pathology, as the name implies, has to do with a diagnosis-and-treatment approach to sickness. It includes all that can (and does) go wrong in human personalities (psychopathology) and relationships. Its focus is upon the symptoms of disease, the marital 'bugs' that get into the system by various routes and cause havoc, pain and unhappiness. This focus is of course vital, since disease in any form represents a health hazard and needs eradication. We will always need the 'marital paramedics' to call upon in the crises of broken relationships. They are the trained counsellors who help to 'stop the bleeding' when two people feel that a DIY approach is no longer working and that outside help has become a necessity.

However, this emphasis on pathology in marriage relationships (necessary as it is) needs to be balanced by the provision of additional resources that are in essence *preventive*. Of the two, it is often said, prevention is better than cure. Far better to stay healthy than become sick.

As if to parallel the modern medical emphasis on prevention of illness and disease through such popular methods as regular screening and cholesterol tests, marriage enrichment has arisen to do the same for marital relationships. The importance of marriage enrichment to the well-being of modern marriage is emphasized by Harold Lief, writing in 1981: 'The marriage enrichment movement, a product of the decade of the 1970s, is growing rapidly, gaining momentum, and will become in my estimation an important social force in the next decade.'[23]

By the 1990s as Dr Lief foretold, interest in marriage enrichment has indeed proliferated, not least in the various branches of the Christian Church which has taken a lead in this movement. Most mainline churches have their own special marriage enrichment programmes. (See Appendix B for details).

On what principles are these programmes based?

6. The Basic Principles

1. Potential for growth

The fundamental principle is the recognition of the potential for growth in a marriage relationship. This challenges at once the outdated notion that marriage is a static state, unchanging and unchangeable. Growth assumes life; and life is forever changing and evolving, moving forwards to face fresh challenges and needs.

The marriage enrichment movement assumes a *dynamic* rather than a *static* view of the marital contract. Marriage does not consist of pieces of paper (marriage certificates), the dry and fading evidence of a contract mutually decided upon. Rather, marriage is understood in terms of an ongoing flow of two lives that have chosen to unite in celebration of their love for one another; it does not depend upon whether or not the couple have chosen to take part in a wedding ceremony. Some recent legislation in the U.K. has taken account of this, and the gap between legal marriages and common-law marriages has now closed considerably. The distinction is no longer seen as exclusive – this is a marriage, this one is not – and similar legal rights are available to the unmarried as to the couples who have participated in a wedding service. Perhaps it would be more helpful if we thought of 'common-law marriages' as ordinary marriages that lacked a wedding ceremony?

It is far more important to recognize that the heart of a marriage consists of a loving commitment to one another rather than a dry legal contract. Love rather than law is the basis of a growing, healthy union.

2. Unconscious factors

Marriage enrichment takes account of the fact that marriage implies a *psychological* contract between husband and wife that includes all the unconscious factors that we bring to that union. It is the failure to take account of these unconscious factors that leads to much misery in marriage. Basically, a psychological contract includes 'all the hidden desires and automatic behaviours that are left over from childhood and that inexorably lead couples into conflict'.[24] Marriage enrichment programmes are designed to take account of this unconscious marriage, and to lead couples towards an uncovering of hidden motives and desires. The past, especially our experience of childhood, is often found to contain the key to unravelling our hidden longings and expectations and all that can get transferred unconsciously on to our partner in the here-and-now.

As I have written briefly elsewhere, there are many unhealthy models of marriage that reflect the hidden 'scripts' brought into our marriage from our childhood.[25] Perhaps the best known is the 'Peter-Pan-and-Wendy' type of marriage; he is very much the 'little boy' and she is the mother-substitute Wendy. Such partnerships are totally unconscious; it is other people who can identify the 'script'. Somehow or other, the Peter Pans and the Wendys of this world often find each other with unerring regularity. She needs someone to mother; he needs someone to look after him, and occasionally it works out fine. It is these unconscious factors that some of the exercises in marriage enrichment are intended to address; the more conscious our marriage becomes the more we are in control of childhood elements which may ultimately destroy the union.

3. Opening up a marriage

A third principle of marriage enrichment is to regard marriages as either open or closed. It emphasizes the following distinction:

> An open system is receptive to change and able to change, and is open to alternative ways of responding to various facets of life. It respects and affirms the worth and value of differences, permits a wide range of feeling responses, and can make flexible adaptations to new inputs. A closed system resists change, has rigid qualities, values conformity and sees differences as a threat, does not value the expression of full range of feelings such as anger, tenderness and sadness, and is relatively incapable of making flexible adaptations to new input.[26]

The classic study by Nena and George O'Neill, quoted earlier (see pp. 12–13), is a brilliant exposition of the dangers inherent in the closed marriage and the opportunities of an enhanced marriage through the adoption of the open style of relating. No one finds this change easy to make, especially if the marriage has been 'closed' for a long time. It must begin with a new and improved style of communication between the couple, and marriage enrichment programmes always include practical experiments by which to improve the freedom of expressing our thoughts, feelings and longings. In brief, the O'Neills suggest a rewriting of the marriage contract, weeding out the things we are either tired of or that have outlived their usefulness, and substituting a new style of open expression more appropriate to the needs of the present. The difference between the two styles of marriage is summarized like this:

The old contract demands:	*The open contract offers*:
ownership of the mate	non-dependent living
denial of the self	personal growth
playing the couples game	individual freedom

rigid role behaviour	flexible roles
absolute fidelity	mutual trust
total exclusivity	expansion through openness

Even with this cryptic summary to go on, you can see how they diverge, and at least provide the outline of an agenda to be discussed in depth by each couple. This leads us to a fourth principle.

4. Freedom to experiment

Marriage enrichment emphasizes the need for freedom to experiment in improving the quality of the marriage.

There can be no improvement in the enjoyment of our marriage without taking the risk of expressing our deepest needs and longings. Marriage enrichment is about 'trying on new styles of relating' in order to enhance the quality of what is already a 'good enough' marriage. It emphasizes the possibility of new experiences through which our marriage and love is enhanced. We may be able to discover new strengths and identify old weaknesses as we risk the open trust of one another in the ongoing adventure of love. Marriage enrichment does not try to 'sell' anything; on the contrary, it is based on giving couples permission to experience a whole range of alternative methods in improving the quality of their marriage. Remember: *There is no law that says that something cannot happen for the first time!*

This emphasis on the freedom to experiment addresses one of the major causes of marital disharmony: *rigidity*. Whether it is expressed in behaviour patterns or in firmly maintained 'sexist' roles and stereotypes, rigidity is the very antithesis of growth and development in marriage. Marriage enrichment addresses the degree to which each partner is satisfied with the 'way things are' in the marriage. This involves putting the whole of the relationship under a microscope, and this can raise some very awkward questions. In the accepting and supportive environment of, say, a marriage enrichment weekend, couples can dare to risk 'trying on' other modes of behaviour more suited to contemporary needs. It encourages a willingness to experiment with alternative styles of behaving, relating and communicating that can act as antidotes to sterility.

5. Learning new skills

Marriage enrichment is educational – teaching new skills in communication, problem solving, and conflict resolution.

Some people interpret 'education' as 'telling me how to run my marriage'! Nothing could be further from the truth. While marriage is one of the greatest commitments that we can ever make, apart from parenthood, we get very little (if any) preparation for it. Some churches have marriage preparation sessions but these are often token offerings and, frankly, most couples would be unwilling to enter into long-term preparation for their marriage.

Education is of little value if we fail to see the relevance of the teaching to our daily experience. It is usually after some experience of married life that the underlying issues and questions arise, and then we are more amenable to learning new methods and skills in relating and communicating.

Nowhere is this more true than in conflict resolution. Many of us have a painful history of conflict, beginning with our childhood experiences, and we grow up tending to avoid conflict like the plague. We see it – as we always used to see it when we were young – as totally negative and always painful. The idea that some experiences of conflict can actually be *creative* might never have occurred to us, that out of 'creative conflict' some improvements can be made to the quality of our most important relationship. Marriage enrichment does not duck this issue. (My first book, *Couples Arguing*, is devoted to the subject of 'fighting fairly', and you may find it useful.)

6. Intimacy

Marriage enrichment is grounded in the importance of intimacy, the heart and soul of any nurturing and resourceful relationship. This goes to the very core of what a marriage is about. It is hardly surprising, considering that the Latin word *intimus* means inner or innermost. It implies knowing a person at the deepest level of their being.

There will always be the risk that some people find this degree of 'knowing' far too threatening for comfort. Others are just longing for deeper experiences of intimacy with their partner and a deeper understanding between them. Again, there is nothing in marriage enrichment that requires people to do anything they do not wish to do. On the contrary, the principles of marriage enrichment are designed so that couples can find in them just what they want, for the present. The emphasis is upon helping couples get what they want from their marriage, and it is up to them to decide upon what level of intimacy they feel most comfortable with. By raising the issue, couples are given the opportunity of examining the subject and can assess to what degree the intimacy factor in their marriage is satisfactory. (The whole of chapter 11 is devoted to this important aspect of marriage enrichment.)

7. Becoming who we are

Marriage enrichment attempts to keep in balance the needs for individual growth as well as the need for the marriage to grow.

Each partner has their own particular needs for growth and development. Yet a 'couple' is a greater reality than the sum of its two (human) parts. There is an extra 'something' when two people relate in an intimate way. A 'relationship' is born out of their mutual trust, love and functioning together as a couple. Both this relationship and the individuals within it need to grow and develop in healthy and constructive ways, and marriage enrichment is aware of both these needs. I need to become more fully who I am, in order that I may have as much of me as I am aware of to give to my wife in our marriage. Jan also needs to become as fully 'self-actualized' as she is capable of, both for her own sake and for the sake of our marriage. This balance between 'self-' and 'relationship-' actualization is an important aspect of marriage enrichment philosophy. While marriage enrichment emphasizes the importance of improving the quality of the marital relationship, 'the ideal base for a marital relationship is that each partner have a strong sense of himself (*sic*) as a separate, whole person, whose survival is attached to himself and to his own growth'.[27]

These seven basic principles provide us with a brief understanding of the foundation upon which the structure of marriage enrichment is based.

The first introduction to the process of marriage enrichment for many couples may be through attending one of the many residential weekends arranged for those who wish to improve the quality of their relationship. (I have included an outline of one couple's experience of a residential marriage enrichment weekend in chapter 13.) Briefly, the weekend provides each couple with the freedom, space, time and opportunity to work on improving their marriage. There is no 'washing dirty linen in public'; couples mostly work by themselves, and any sharing is for each couple to decide when meeting in the larger groups. The word coming from such marriage enrichment programmes is very positive indeed, although there are bound to be some natural fears and objections to any new venture. Marriage enrichment cannot be excluded from such criticisms; here are a few to consider.

7. Some Objections Considered

In spite of it being an entirely voluntary activity, there are those who would criticize the entire project. Briefly, the criticisms concern the following:

'*The whole idea is far too introspective!*'
It is true that the process does involve an invitation to explore the unexplored parts of their relationship, to roll up the matrimonial carpet and find out what is underneath. For some people that prospect would be an enormous risk. The alternative, however, is to allow the carpet to rise higher and higher as unresolved issues and conflicts get swept underneath until the strain of keeping the carpet on the floor becomes impossible.

'*Isn't the whole thing far too threatening for the average marriage?*'
Frankly, it could be, depending on how you define the average marriage. Some couples might prefer to continue as they have always done rather than face what may be an embarrassing and uncomfortable experience of putting a spotlight on their marriage. That is a choice for each couple to make. The prospect of a better marriage makes this threat a viable choice for thousands of people today. It has to be remembered, however, that marriage enrichment is usually appropriate only where there already exists a high degree of stability in the marriage that is capable of sustaining such an examination.

'Supposing two people find out they want different things out of their marriage? Haven't you then done more harm than good?'
Again, no one is forcing anyone to do or change anything. If a couple find out they want different things out of their marriage there is no point in hiding the fact. It may be better to find out sooner rather than later what these things are, and to discover to what extent the fulfilment of these needs are both possible and acceptable within the present marriage. Marriage enrichment is about making choices.

'What would the neighbours say?'
That depends on your neighbours! They could be thrilled by the idea and express an interest in coming to a marriage enrichment weekend with you. To go for a health check is no longer regarded as the activity of 'health freaks'. To go for a check-up on your marriage need not be identified with some weird activity, other than by those whose own marriage would not bear scrutiny. Enrichment does not bear the same stigma as 'therapy', since enrichment does not assume anything to be wrong with the marriage.

'Leave well alone!'
Yes, if ignorance is bliss, then do so. This 'Little-Bo-Peep' attitude (remember? 'Leave them alone and they'll come home, wagging their tails behind them') may hold some attractions, but if there are serious undiagnosed issues underneath a seemingly good-enough marriage, it might be more prudent to know what they are and take appropriate action while there is time.

'What if my partner disagrees with marriage enrichment?'
If you have discussed the possibility of attending a marriage enrichment weekend with your partner and they refuse to go with you, this does rule out the prospect, since it is a joint activity. Perhaps you could gently enquire what their hesitations or objections are and try to answer them as best as you can. Don't they want their present good relationship

to be improved upon? This could lead to a profitable conversation concerning your partner's feelings and how they view the marriage. This of itself might be useful.

'I'm not going to wash our dirty linen in public!'
Most marriage enrichment programmes have opportunities for working as a couple, so that for most of the time you are working with one another. There may, depending on the agency providing the service, be open sessions – growth groups – where couples could work with their partner in the context of a whole group. The advantage of working with other couples is that you discover you are not the only ones having problems with embarrassment or honesty! The educational value of such a programme is enhanced by having more than your own experience to go on, and this wider experience can be extremely valuable to all the couples in the programme. You are responsible for what you choose to bring up in such 'open' groups, and anything you would find it hard to handle in public need not be divulged. There are always opportunities for raising such matters in a private session with the programme leaders.

It is perfectly usual for couples to feel nervous about going to enrichment weekends, but attendance is not necessary to the application of the principles of marriage enrichment to your marriage. Books such as this can provide you with enough material to work on for the time being.

If you are going to apply these principles, how might you go about it? I want to devote the rest of the book to this important aspect of how you could implement these insights to the improvement of your most important relationship – the survival of the long-distance marriage.

PART 4

Marriage Enrichment in Practice

8. Listening and Responding

Introduction

As we begin to apply the principles in the previous chapter, we enter into the important and sometimes difficult aspect of marriage enrichment, namely, knowing and stating what we want for ourselves.

It is so easy to get into the habit of deferring to the wishes and needs of our partner, that our own needs get submerged in the interest of marital harmony. Others, of course, habitually ignore the needs of their partner.

There can be no continuing enrichment until we face the question: How can I get what I want out of my marriage without appearing to be totally selfish? Is the way of 'self-denial' always a good thing? As we noticed (pp. 27–29) false notions of 'self-denial' can often cloud the issue of improving the quality of a marriage. Indeed, some people may say that denying their own needs in marriage is the reason it has survived for so long! Expressing what we want, it is suggested, will only make matters worse. If partners started to become vocal about what they expected from their marriage, may not the fat get into the fire? I believe a more healthy way would involve an honest sharing by each partner of their expectations of their marriage. This will involve the vital matter of listening.

An exercise in listening

So, just pause for a moment, and ask yourself this question (it may help to do this with your partner): 'If I could have one wish concerning my marriage, what would it be?'

The fact that you have wished for something indicates a number of things:

1. Your marriage is still alive!
2. You are aware of at least one area in which you would like to see some improvement.
3. You are brave enough to allow yourself to name this thing.

You will need to convey this wish to your partner, and indeed to hear their wish too. When you share this – as with all the exercises – please do not get into discussions. Just listen! Receiving another person's wish is a very privileged thing and needs to be handled gently. Responses such as:

> 'That's ridiculous!'
> 'Don't be stupid!'
> 'That's asking for the moon!'
> 'You're never satisfied!'
> 'How do you think that makes me feel?'
> 'Thousands of people would give their eye teeth for a marriage like ours!'
> 'Do you think I'm made of money?'

are extremely unhelpful. Make it clear to your partner that you are not making any demands upon them, nor indicating any inadequacy in them. You are merely expressing – in a fanciful kind of way – what your wish for your marriage might be. You are not, at this stage, *asking* for anything. You are beginning to give yourself permission to dream dreams.

Supposing your wish is for more contentment or security, or less time spent apart. You are drawing attention both to yourself and to your partner, of an awareness of a single issue which could improve your enjoyment of what you already have.

HE:	I wish for more physical contact with you.	(*The husband tells his wife his wish*)
SHE:	You wish for more physical contact with me.	(*Wife repeats the wish of her husband*)

This simple exercise is called 'mirroring' and establishes that you have been heard accurately.

I think some of you may find such an exchange completely unreal. 'Do couples ever talk like that?' you may understandably ask. I have to say that the fact that they do not is one of the biggest causes of frustration in marriage. The usual responses to the expression of any wish is likely to be those mentioned above: denial, confrontation, ridicule, threats and exasperation.

The sad fact is that very few of us have formed the habit of hearing what our partners are actually saying. If marriages are to be improved there must be more attention paid by partners to listening to each other. In a Gallup Poll (June 1990), 56 per cent of the sample gave 'never listens to me' as a major source of tension within their marriage.[28] Unfortunately, most of us have lost the knack of really paying attention to what our partner is trying to tell us. Their voice becomes part of a background noise, which we simply filter out while doing something else. If we do hear them, we may only do so in order to make our own counter-attack – which is another way of not listening to what they are saying. We enrich our marriage when we make a commitment to hear what our partner is trying to say. Repeating it back to them reinforces the fact that we have heard what they say. We can disagree or argue about what they are saying later, but initially we need to assure them that we are hearing accurately what they say.

Let us take this exercise in listening one stage further and illustrate how it can be developed into a useful dialogue between partners. Having expressed your wish to your partner, and having had it repeated back to you so that you are sure they have heard, you can do the same with their wish. It may be:

SHE:	I wish we could spend more time together.	(*Wife expresses her wish*)
HE:	You'd like me to spend more time with you.	(*The husband repeats his wife's wish*)

Again, the important point is that the husband must pay attention to what his wife is saying, and 'feed' it back to her in such a way that she is convinced that what she has said has been received. This is not the moment to argue the point, or to launch a counter-attack.

Because the needs of each partner are important to the continued growth and enjoyment of the marriage, they now need to be explored more fully together, with a view to discovering how, and to what extent, these important 'wishes' can be fulfilled.

Implementing the wishes of both partners

One at a time, the needs that lie behind these wishes can now be more fully examined. The conversation may proceed along these lines:

SHE:	You say you'd like more physical contact with me. I'd like you to say a bit more about that.	(*This is the important phase of EXPLORATION. Then comes the need for UNDERSTANDING*)
HE:	I wonder if you notice that when I put my arm around you, you sometimes shrug me off?	(*The specifics of his need are now spelled out.*)

SHE: No, I've not been aware of that; maybe it's a habit. I really don't mean to reject you.	(*She is now showing some AWARENESS of her behaviour.*)

Some useful responses to the wishes and needs of our partner are:

'Can you say a bit more about what you mean?'
'I'm not sure I follow you.'
'Tell me more about that.'
'How do you feel about that?'

The importance of such responses is that they get away from the possible rebuttal of such expressions of need. We can become so defensive when our partner expresses a need, that we immediately feel attacked. Instead of exploring what our partner is trying to tell us we launch the counter-attack about their short-comings. Responses such as those above are intended to 'hold our fire' and, instead, to explore more fully what our partner is trying to make us aware of.

A regular diet of such interaction does much to improve the quality of our union. Listening shows that we *care*, and that the needs of our partner matter. Similarly, by expressing our own needs to our partner we make the point that we too have needs that must be addressed from time to time. As with weeds, *to leave a problem is to increase a problem*. Many couples have developed a very positive way of dealing with such matters, but others are either too afraid or too self-conscious to raise them.

Listening to our partner at this 'attentive' level, and responding to them openly with a desire to explore their needs, is one sign of a living, growing relationship.

Awareness exercise

In order to increase your self-awareness, try completing the following sentences. Be as honest as you can with yourself.

I (always/sometimes/never) express my wishes or preferences in my marriage. This is because ....
....

I (always/sometimes/never) find it hard to express my feelings. This is because ....
....

If I told my partner what I wanted he/she would ....
....

When my partner expresses their wishes or preferences I usually ....
....

When I don't express my needs directly I try to get them met by ....
....

Out of a total of 10, I would assess my partner's ability to hear me correctly as (ring one)
10 9 8 7 6 5 4 3 2 1 0,
and because of that I feel ....
....

Whenever I feel unheard, I usually react by ....
....

Instead of allowing my partner to get away with not hearing me, I could ....
....

Try sharing your completed sentences with your partner as a way of practising listening and responding.

The question of time and timing

Timing is an important issue when raising subjects for discussion with our partner. It is obviously very little use doing this over breakfast when (in the average home) everyone is trying to get ready to go out for the day, and the home resembles Piccadilly Circus in the rush hour!

You may need to mark off some time in the family diary or schedule quite deliberately. I recall the vicar whose wife rang from a local call-box anonymously in order to arrange a time to see him. Imagine his feelings when he opened the vicarage door – to his wife! Desperate problems often require desperate remedies. It may not be so bad in your family, but at least it shows the lengths to which some people are driven in order to get a hearing from their partner. Don't imagine that, somehow or other, you will *find* the time. Many couples don't find the time: they have to *make* it.

Listening to our partners in depth requires undivided attention. That means no papers, no TV or videos flickering in the corner of the room to which attention can drift. I recall in my parish ministry many occasions when, calling for some specific reason like a baptism or funeral, I was plonked down in the corner of the room while the family communicated to me watching the TV the whole time. In the end, I used to refuse their offer of a seat, and stand myself in front of the screen. They usually got the message! Nowadays, I'd be a bit more direct.

Eye contact can be a very threatening experience for some people. However, there is nothing quite like it for giving and receiving attention. Embarrassment there may be; but this may be a small price to pay for getting your message across to your partner.

In 'good enough' marriages there will usually be a good deal of in-depth listening going on already. You may, by now, have discovered very adequate methods of gaining your partner's attention. It could even be that your life is such that these times can be arranged without too much hassle or artificiality. Joint activities can provide natural occasions for open sharing, even if it is over the washing-up or the emptying of the dish-washer. Walks, car rides, bed-times, all provide natural pauses during the day when issues can be raised and feelings aired. It is best done at a time when children are not around, since their presence may inhibit the free and open expression of what you want to say to your partner. Quality time is essential to the ongoing growth of a union.

Excuses

There are many excuses used to prevent open communication with our partners:

She may say:

He is so busy.
I don't like to bother him.
He is so tired.
I'm sure it can wait.
He never listens to me anyway!
(sigh) What difference will it make anyway?
I hate to add to his troubles.
Maybe it's not so important after all?
It may cause more problems if I say anything.

He may say:

She's too busy.
She's had a hard day with the kids.
I'll say something tomorrow.
It's not all that important anyway.
I can't say anything when she looks so washed out.
What good would it do anyway – she'll never change.
When she sits down, she falls asleep!
Let sleeping dogs lie.
My needs can wait.

Most of these responses are blatant excuses. Under the guise of caring for our partner, we are in fact protecting ourselves. As we noticed earlier in the case of Peter and Pauline, self-interest can easily be disguised as care for the other.

Studies of human behaviour teach us that when a legitimate need gets suppressed or avoided, it doesn't just go away. We may have forgotten it, but it has not forgotten us! Somewhere, deep inside us, that need gets to work on finding another way of expressing itself.

If legitimate needs cannot find expression openly they will sneak out in underhanded ways instead. Take anger as an example.

Anger

Anger is one of our strongest emotions and, surprising as it may appear, is essentially 'user-friendly'. Our anger is one of the ways we protect ourselves. Sam Keen identifies with his own anger and sees its advantages:

> I keep you safe by making your full strength available to you in situations of danger. I help you to identify those enemies that threaten your well-being. I defend the boundaries of the physical, psychological, economic and social space you need to survive . . . I keep one person from being swallowed up by another and thus preserve the duality which is necessary for love. If you doubt that I am the companion of love, remember the ecstasy of the reconciliation that comes after fighting. After a good expression of clean anger, lovers have established the integrity of their separateness, and they may come together without fearing that either will be eradicated by the act of love. If you can't fight, you can't love.[29]

Providing our anger comes out directly it can help us to defend our boundaries and to express our strongest emotions so that our partner can know how we feel. Such direct expressions of anger can actually help to strengthen our marriage, because we are levelling with one another in honesty and straightforwardness. But if we do not allow ourselves to express our anger directly, it usually comes out in some other way. Denied egress through the 'front door', it must now seek sneaky ways of expression by seeping out of the 'back door' where we may have little or no control over it. For example, sarcasm is one such veiled form of anger.

Sarcasm is what we resort to when we do not use our anger directly. Think of how you use, or are the recipient of other people's, sarcasm. It comes out as a twisted form of humour. If you are late, they may say to you, 'Punctual, as usual!' When hurt, they may say, 'Why don't you say something really hurtful?' These are veiled, subversive ways of expressing really angry feelings, and they do much to destroy the beauty of any relationship. It really does pay to get angry, directly and to the point. Some of us need to learn appropriate ways of expressing our anger. Here is a way to get you started. Try completing the following sentences:

I feel really angry when ....
....

I don't express my anger to you because ....
....

If I were to get really angry with you then ....
....

When you get angry with me I feel ....
....

Instead of getting angry with you I ....
....

I'd prefer your real anger to your sarcasm because ....
....

Sometimes I get angry with myself and then I ....
....

I'm frightened by anger because ....
....

In my childhood, anger meant ....
....

When my parents expressed anger, I would always feel .....
....

Not all these statements will fit everybody, but they may suggest ways of getting the subject of anger on to the marriage agenda and discussing how it can be dealt with more constructively in the future. You may care to discuss with your partner Sam Keen's dictum: 'If you can't fight, you can't love'.

It is just as important to discover why anger is never openly expressed in a marriage as to discover why one partner is perpetually angry. There is usually something else going on when either of these two extreme situations are in operation.

Opening ourselves up to our feelings

Some couples pride themselves on never getting angry with their partners. Such marriages can be among the most stable in our families. What lies behind this pride?

It can, of course, be total collusion: 'I won't express my anger if you don't express yours.' While this may never have been said openly, some 'truce' like this may be operating under the surface of the marriage. For two people, who have lived together for forty or fifty years, never to have been angry with each other stretches our credulity. In such cases I ask myself, 'What on earth have they done with their natural anger?' Or, 'Is the union so fragile that one argument might end it all?' Argument-free marriages are not always as healthy as they may appear on the surface. Somewhere along the marital line it is highly possible that one or other of the partners has been continually giving way in the interests of peace and quiet.

We may also ask, 'If they have not been expressing their anger directly and verbally, what non-verbal messages have they been giving out in terms of "body language"?'

Body language

We all know that looks can kill! Without a word being spoken, a single arched eyebrow can demolish us. A friend arrives who invites the husband round to the pub for a drink. He instinctively looks at his wife, who has a disapproving scowl on her face. He then makes an excuse not to go. Without a word being spoken, he has received a very clear 'message' from his wife that his visit to the pub would not be approved of and, if he did go, it might end up with reprisals being taken later. Such reprisals would not be out in the open; but the wife's silences or headaches would be clear indications of her disapproval and a means of bringing the husband to heel once more.

Such couples would swear blind that they never have rows! With body language like that around, who needs words? There is such a thing as a 'pleaser' marriage, wherein the silent understanding is, 'I won't upset you if you don't upset me.' While the partners in such marriages pride themselves on its strength ('We don't have arguments in our marriage!') there are in fact some fundamental weaknesses that are not being addressed.

We can deal more appropriately with such issues by inviting the body language into a verbal expression, like this:

> 'You seem not to want me to go to the pub?'
> 'Don't you want me to go to the pub?'
> 'Tell me what your scowl is about.'
> 'If you'd rather I didn't go, I wish you would say so!'
> 'You don't seem happy about the idea.'
> 'If you want me to stay in, just say so!'
> 'How do you feel about me going to the pub?'

Of course, body language does not only consist of angry looks. There are also shrugs, smiles and tears, sadness and laughter, which can be invited into a verbal expression.

Mind-reading

In some marriages there is an oft-repeated phrase, 'If you really loved me, I wouldn't have to tell you what I need.' This can take place in what I call the 'Rumpelstiltskin marriage'. In the famous fairy story a father, anxious to impress the king, tells him that his daughter can spin gold out of straw. When put to the test, of course, she cannot do it. But a strange little man appears each night and spins the straw into gold – for a price. When all the girl's jewellery has gone, she has nothing more to offer – and the king's demands get bigger and bigger each night. Eventually, she agrees to give the little man her first child, never believing that she will have to fulfil her pledge. Finally, the king marries the girl and upon the birth of her first child the strange little man reappears and demands that she fulfils her promise. When she pleads for mercy, the little man says she can keep her child only if she can guess his name. Of course she cannot do this, until one of her messengers overhears the little man dancing in the forest, singing to himself, 'Rumpelstiltskin is my name.'

Whenever we act out such 'guessing games' in our marriage, we are placing an enormous strain upon them. The phrase, 'If you really loved me I wouldn't have to tell you what I need!' is a dishonest way of avoiding being open about our needs and telling our partner what they are. It may sound like a high standard of intimacy wherein we can read the minds of our partners, but in reality *it places all the responsibility for getting our needs met upon the other person.*

When this Rumpelstiltskin kind of marriage has been operating for some time, couples can often feel guilty when they fail to read the prevailing signs correctly. This merely adds extra strain to the relationship, all the energy going into discerning what the other partner is thinking, feeling and needing. It operates on a series of 'nods and winks', with an occasional 'nudge-nudge' just to push the message home. The result of this kind of behaviour is to place the relationship under perpetual tension. For we can never be sure that we have read the 'signs' correctly. We do not have to become mind-readers, whereby we have to guess what our partner is thinking, feeling or wanting.

Expectations of mind-reading also give all the power in the marriage to the partner who is playing this kind of marital game. Not to make a sexual advance can be met with, 'Have I got to send you a letter?' while to make a sexual advance can be met with, 'Don't you realize I've had a heavy day?' The actual message is, 'I won't ever let you get it right.'

Many marriages are eventually destroyed by this kind of marital game. The pressure gets too great; the tension becomes unbearable. Depression or breakdown can be the result of this pernicious kind of brainwashing. To prevent this from happening in the first place, we need to have access to a formula by which we can break through such 'mind-reading' games. Here are a few to get you started:

'I am not a mind-reader.'
'Please say what you want.'
'How can I please you if you won't tell me your needs?'
'I'm tired of these guessing games.'
'If you want something, just ask.'
'What would you prefer?'
'Why didn't you say?'
'I feel angry when you expect me to read your mind.'
'If you won't say, of course I'm likely to get it wrong.'
'You don't always read my mind; why should I read yours?'
'Let's be honest with each other about what we feel.'
'It's OK to say what you want.'
'Give yourself permission to say what you need.'
'I'd rather know what you want.'

I am aware that no two people can live together for any length of time without them developing a kind of 'sixth sense'. It is lovely when someone brings you a cup of tea just as you are thinking how thirsty you are! This kind of thing happens quite naturally when there is no game-playing but just a quiet sensitivity to the needs of the other person. This is a different kind of activity to that mentioned above. In 'mind-reading' games, the onus is placed upon the other partner; in a sensitive relationship we take responsibility for ourselves. It arises out of wanting to express our love and our caring for our partner, but it will always be open to 'checking out' that we have correctly discerned the needs of our partner.

Expressing appreciation

The need for saying 'thank you' to our partner may sound too obvious for words; but how often do we overlook the obvious? Regular expressions of appreciation are like rays of sunshine that lighten up the marriage relationship and make it worth while. Many relationships cool down for lack of such expressions, and this can give rise to the destructive pattern of taking our partners for granted. Our gratitude can become part of the 'mind-reading' game mentioned earlier, whereby it could be said, 'Of course you know I'm grateful for what you do. Do I have to spell it out?' The true answer is, 'Yes, you do.' We need to hear thanks given regularly so that we are assured that our efforts towards the marital harmony and smooth working of the partnership continue to be felt worthwhile.

On a scale of 10, where do you and your partner come in saying 'Thank you'? (ring)

MINE:	1	2	3	4	5	6	7	8	9	10
HIS/HERS:	1	2	3	4	5	6	7	8	9	10

Would you like any improvements made? If so, how could you do this?

Summary

In this chapter, we have considered the important role that listening and responding have in a marriage. We have identified some excuses that are used to conceal our feelings, especially angry feelings. The important question of time and timing in our self-expression needs to be explored in any growing partnership. We have seen how silence is often used as a means of 'keeping the peace' but in fact perpetuates the war. 'Not saying' can be used as a weapon, and this comes out in the way in which we allow our bodies and our looks to convey our feelings. It also gives rise to the 'mind-reading' games which place all the responsibility on the other person for meeting our needs. While a growing, sensitive awareness of our partner's needs usually comes with time, this does not absolve each partner from the responsibility of stating their feelings and their needs when occasion demands. The ability and willingness to express our appreciation of one another is an important aspect of a growing marriage, whereby we experience the worthwhileness of our efforts; this prevents the growth of negative feelings associated with being taken for granted.

9. Assessing Role Expectations

Key to growth

One of the most important determining factors to the success of any marriage is its capacity to grow. That means its ability *to face change creatively*.

To understand marriage as a static state, as we have noted above, is to deny it success from the outset. Marriages are comprised of two volatile elements: human beings. As much as we may like to dream of an unchanging state of bliss in our marriage, this is rarely achieved. If it is achieved, it is at the cost of encountering anything new. The only place I know of where there is an unchanging state of bliss is the graveyard – hardly a promising model for any marriage.

However, it would be easy, and cheap, to dismiss such dreams as unreal. They are based, however, on our ordinary human need for stability and security. Indeed, many people marry for precisely those reasons. While it is popular to wish to view the state of marriage as unchanging (and we have already noticed reasons to question this premise), the elements of a marriage, viz. two ordinary human beings, are certainly far from unchanging. We age. We change. We mature. We face a changing world to which we need to adapt. On the basis of the survival of the fittest, only those capable of adaptation survive. So our dreams of a static-state marriage are doomed from the outset. In fact, such fantasies often create the very circumstances that destroy any hope of a permanent union.

Harville Hendrix writes:

> Marriage is not a static state between two unchanging people. Marriage is a psychological and spiritual journey that begins in the ecstasy of attraction, meanders through a rocky stretch of self-discovery, and culminates in the creation of an intimate, joyful, lifelong union.[30]

As the human lifespan increases, so modern marriages have to endure a long 'shelf-life'. One of the reasons for the increasing failure of marriages is the reluctance to take this fact into account at the outset. Most people getting married today see no further than getting the home established, keeping their jobs, and paying off the mortgage. Some may look ahead to the day when they may have children, but that is thought of as in some long-distant future. However, there may be forty or fifty years of marriage ahead of them, and the degree to which they will succeed in their marriage is directly related to their attitude to change.

As we proceed into the 1990s, one of the chief focal points of change concerns the role of men in marriage. The 1970s and 1980s may have seen a breath-taking revolution concerning the role and status of women, but for the 1990s the role of men appears to be at the top of the social agenda. The shorthand term, popular in the media today, is 'the New Man'.

The 'New Man'

Writing in *The Observer* (11 Feb 1990), Yvonne Roberts refers to *The Mintel Report* (February 1990) which says that, in the 1990s, 'a more home-orientated New Man will regard domesticity as an acceptable stripe of promotion from the rank of Robot-Workaholic to that of Warm Well-Rounded Human Being'. This may not be gained (as women see it) without a battle, and a certain amount of resentment. Yet, faced with unemployment or part-time work, some men are entering the unfamiliar world of the kitchen, microwave ovens, washing-machine programmes and the paralysing display of washing powders in the supermarket – and are learning to like it!

The 1990s New Man is rather hard to define as he is still in the design stage. It is not yet possible to say how the finished product will look. What can be said with certainty, however, is that he will be characterized not merely by new actions but particularly by new *attitudes*. These attitudes will concern three vital areas: work, domesticity and child-rearing.

New attitudes

Work

As more women pour into the labour market in the wake of a fall in the availability of school-leavers, the traditionally safe male preserves at work will be under more severe attack than ever before. Yvonne Roberts says, '[Women] will be trying to outstrip men outside the home as well.' She believes they will 'hurtle after promotion and strain for the first cardiac arrest precisely at a time when men have begun to realize that that kind of "success" is not worth having'. A working woman means a more independent woman, and recent UK changes in the provision of separate income-tax assessment have reinforced that independence. The New Man will welcome this and not feel threatened by it; interdependence rather than dependence characterizes the New Woman, and this has repercussions on traditionally hide-bound marriages where the male has held the ultimate purse-strings.

Domesticity

On the domestic front, there may be more house-husbands than hitherto. They are by no means a new species but they are likely to become more familiar and acceptable. With greater opportunities for women to reach the higher echelons of commercial, industrial and academic arenas, some men may find a new lease of life within the home. This is likely, says Ms. Roberts, to attract some flak from women. 'It comes', she says, 'in the form of hints that nothing he does is quite good enough. The laundry is grey; the ironing has creases; the iceberg lettuce he buys should be cos; and when in hell does he think the family will eat five tins of haggis?' This may represent a new form of crisis for marriages when women, for a change, will have to put up with what the husband chooses to cook for the evening meal!

Child-rearing

Children will increasingly become the responsibility of both parents, not just the female of the partnership. A colleague told me recently of a visit he made with one of his daughters to the doctor's surgery. The doctor said, 'Tell your wife to give her three of these tablets a day, and one dose of the other medicine before she goes to sleep at night.' My friend was furious. But this was but a small taste of what women have been receiving for years. The doctor's assumption was that the wife was the matron-in-charge of tablets and that the man would not understand how a medical regimen works. Sexism still reigns but its bastions are going to come under a more concentrated attack in the 1990s. This time the New Man is not going to be left behind. Sexism against *men* is coming under closer scrutiny. Why, for instance, should baby-changing facilities be provided only in women's toilets? The New Man is going to be as familiar with the insides of supermarkets, vacuum cleaners and E numbers as his female counterpart. His picture has even appeared on the cover of the *Mothercare* catalogue, so at least one marketing manager believes in the New Father!

Political implications

Some of the implications of the rise of the New Man are political. Why should children of single working men be given a higher priority for a place at a local nursery than those of working women? Why should it be assumed that a man is in charge of the family budget, the mortgage and the bank accounts, while the woman's sphere is confined to babies and the kitchen and knowing what day the dustman calls?

Far more significant, however, is the influence national government is having (or considered to have) upon family life. In a Gallup Poll (June 1990) only 13 per cent believed that the Tory government 'believes in the family and is doing all it can'. 40 per cent believed that the government 'claims to believe in the family but is actually weakening it (the figure was 45 per cent among the 18–34 age-group and among those with children at home).[31] The abolition of tax allowances for families with children and the freezing of the child benefit were two factors influencing these opinions. At the time of writing several suggestions are being canvassed at government level concerning the improvement of their record on family care, including the enforcement of maintenance payments direct from the father's employers. It may even turn out that before a decree absolute can be issued such provision of maintenance should be seen as watertight. The Law Commission has put forward such proposals (Nov. 1990).

Where does this leave the New Man? Women are suggesting that, if he does exist, he should be placed on the list of endangered species. Polly Toynbee writes:

> I have heard tell of the New Man. For many years now there have been books and articles proclaiming his advent, even his arrival. I have met women who claim that their sons will be he, or that their daughters may marry him. I have met men who claim they are he. False prophets all, the New Man is not here, and it does not seem likely that we shall see him in our lifetime.[32]

But is it possible that such doubts reveal a reluctance to surrender the hitherto exclusive female bastions to men? Many women would say, 'Give me half a chance!' But for others to surrender their kitchen and their babies to their husbands may be a hard price to pay for their newly won freedom.

Such speculations, however, provide a useful introduction to thinking about the way things are managed in your own marriage. What are the role expectations underlying your own relationship with your partner?

An examination of existing role expectations

This important aspect of marriage enrichment has as its object: 'To identify, express and learn to negotiate or renegotiate role expectations, and to increase the ability to cope creatively with conflict.'[33]

Most marriages apparently run on an outdated and unexamined (male) assumption that the *status quo* is working to the mutual satisfaction of both partners. But what used to work well can become obsolete as circumstances and people change. Unless such changes are made conscious, and the old marital agenda either updated or scrapped, the danger is that hidden resentments creep in and gradually undermine the quality of the relationship. The roles we play in a marriage need regular check-ups to ensure that they are contemporary with our own self-awareness and need for self-fulfilment. Our partners also need to understand our reasons for wanting to change them. The following is one possible way of revising our roles and checking them out with our partner.

Assessment exercise

In the Marital Role Expectations exercise on p. 73 are listed a variety of possible roles we may play within a marriage. The purpose of the exercise is to help you and your partner to discover some of the hidden assumptions upon which your marriage is based, and either to affirm them or, if you don't like these assumptions, negotiate to change them.

First of all just read the exercise through. You will see there is space to add any more roles which you consider important to you but which are not included in the list. Also, delete any that do not apply to your situation.

MARITAL ROLE EXPECTATIONS			
His	*Hers*	*Role title*	*Description of role*
—	—	Homemaker	Responsibility for home life
—	—	Decision maker	Responsibility for decisions affecting family
—	—	Moral/spiritual leader	Carries the responsibility for the religious or ethical values of the family
—	—	Houseworker	Care and maintenance of the house
—	—	Money manager	Arrangements for the family budget
—	—	Sex partner	Understanding and owning one's own sexuality and that of your partner
—	—	Helper	Assisting partner with their work, domestic, business or leisure
—	—	Mother/father	Involvement as parent
—	—	Breadwinner	Amount contributed to family income through work
—	—	Companion	Relating to partner as friend and confidante
—	—	Host/hostess	Involvement in entertaining friends
—	—	Source of love	Giving love to partner and family
—	—	Good citizen	Involvement in wider community work
—	—	Gender model	Expressing appropriate (male/female) behaviour and feelings for family
—	—	Peacemaker	Role in family conflicts
—	—	Child-rearing	Interaction with and responsibility for children
—	—	Lover	Responsibility for increasing the areas of intimacy in the marriage
—	—	....	(here add any roles
—	—	....	important to you but not
—	—	....	included above)

To get the most out of this exercise, try working through the steps as suggested below.

Step 1:

Against 'His' (if you are the man) or 'Hers' (if the woman) try to assess – in order of priority – what you think your partner at present expects of you. There are seventeen possible roles, plus any you have added. Now, try to number these roles in order of priority *as you think your partner sees you*. For instance, if female, you may think your partner sees your chief role as Homemaker; while, if male, you may think you are seen as the Breadwinner. Continue right through the list. It may be that you feel your partner puts equal priority on some of the roles expected of you (e.g. Homemaker, Peacemaker, Houseworker). If so, you can group some of the roles within a smaller number of priorities. There is no right or wrong way of doing the exercise, so don't use up too much energy trying to 'get it right'.

Step 2:

Ask your partner to go through the list using the same criteria as you did in Step 1. (But first place a piece of paper over your numbering in order not to influence him or her.)

Step 3:

When you have both completed your assessment of what your partner's role expectations of you are, share these with one another, as openly and honestly as you can – how each of you *feels* about these expectations that your partner thinks you place on him (or her). To assist in this process, here are some questions you may like to ask one another:

> What surprises you about what you have just discovered?
> What depresses you about what you have just discovered?
> How do you feel about my expectations of you?
> How do you feel about your expectations of me?

What changes would you like to make?
Are you aware of any resentment or anger?

Step 4:
Arising out of Step 3, you are now invited to revise these role expectations according to *how you would like them to be for yourself.* If, for instance, you would like to see your role as 'Sex partner' rated higher in priority than, say, 'Breadwinner', renumber the roles accordingly. Go through the list again, and renumber them according to *your own* preferences and priorities. When you have both done this, you will have discovered a very important 'map' for the future of your marriage. You will find how your expectations of one another have differed – maybe for some time – without either of you being aware of this. You will also have discovered where much of the existing tension, if not conflict, has been coming from, since both of you may have been following different 'maps' and, inevitably, reaching different conclusions.

You may have found that you wish to revise the order of priority of some of these roles within your marriage. A final list could look something like this:

In order of priority, I would like to be –
1. Companion – Lover – Sex partner
2. Helper – Homemaker – Source of love
3. Decision maker – Parent – Gender model
4. House worker – Money manager – Breadwinner
5. Peacemaker – Host/Hostess
6. Moral/Spiritual leader
7. Good citizen

This way of completing the exercise may be seen as more realistic than a straight choice between seventeen roles.

Renegotiation

The object of this exercise is 'to identify, express and learn to negotiate or renegotiate role expectations and to increase the ability to cope creatively with conflict'. (p. 72) This is one of the urgent tasks which long-term marriages especially need to address.

The task of renegotiating the role expectations within a partnership or family does a number of important things:

1. It establishes *flexibility* within the relationship.
2. It improves the quality of *communication* within the marriage.
3. It precludes *gender stereotypes* – 'this is man's/woman's work'.
4. It *re-evaluates* the distribution of labour and input into the family well-being.
5. It can *prevent resentments* from going unnoticed.
6. It maintains the *principle of control* over the way the marriage is managed.
7. It can reveal *hidden assumptions* that have not been checked out to both partners' satisfaction.
8. It supplies *a valuable forum for the expression of justifiable grievances.*
9. It *increases the quality of intimacy* within the marriage as the partners feel themselves valued and cared for.
10. It *prevents the erosion of love* by unthinking behaviour.

Here are some very important aspects of marriage enrichment. Their very openness ensures that marriages do not get set in concrete, unchanging and unchangeable. A regular 'marriage review' – certainly on the occasion of any major change in the marriage – can ensure that the love and trust between couples continues to flow. Examples of such changes are given on pp. 95–6.

In this renegotiation process conflict may arise as role expectations are revised or a suggestion made that they should be changed and updated to meet more contemporary needs. How can such conflict be handled creatively? In other words, how can such renegotiation be managed so that we do not do more harm than good to a basically sound relationship?

Creative conflict

It is understandable that the words 'creative' and 'conflict' are often seen to stand in total opposition. How can conflict ever be a *creative* process? Surely, by definition, conflict is destructive, harmful, confrontational and, in essence, hostile? Is not the common cultural maxim, 'Don't argue!', good advice?

Many people hold to this view, and it is not hard to find the reasons why. I recall taking part in a live radio 'phone-in' programme which was linked up to Dublin. I had just published *Couples Arguing* and listeners were invited to ring in to share experiences. One man berated me; in essence he was saying that I was talking a load of rubbish by claiming that arguing could be a creative process. I asked him what his earliest memories of arguing were, and he went on to share his own very personal and painful memories of the destructive rows which took place in his home when his father came home drunk. He vowed he would never inflict that pain upon his family when he grew up, and has bent over backwards ever since to 'keep the peace'.

None of us come to the subject of 'arguing' from a neutral position. Our past experiences have taught us either how to use the process or, more often, to avoid it if we possibly can. But no process should be judged by its worst excesses. Just because arguments and disagreements lead to violence in some families, it is not necessarily an inevitable outcome in *every* family. One bad apple need not put us off fruit for life.

The problem, as I see it, is that we have so very few examples and experiences of 'good arguments' or 'creative conflict'. I need not repeat here the examples of creative arguing contained in my earlier book,[34] but they may be worth looking at if you would like to see how creative conflict can turn out in practice. Consider, for the moment, these positive advantages in *not* avoiding marital conflict:

1. To identify an issue between you and your partner is different from creating one. It already exists, and to recognize the existence of a problem is half the battle towards solving it.
2. Not to share with your partner something that is a problem to you is to rob your partner of the opportunity of helping to solve it.
3. Avoiding conflict is to prolong the grievance you justifiably feel. You cannot logically blame your partner for an issue s/he knows nothing about.
4. If you avoid confronting an issue with your partner, as may occur in the renegotiating process mentioned above, you must take responsibility for prolonging your sense of hurt or pain.
5. The avoidance of conflict is a major cause of barriers building up between married people. Barriers block off intimacy.
6. Confronting an issue and confronting your partner need not necessarily be the same thing. Confronting an issue can be a joint venture, using your combined energies and insight in order to remove the cause of your concern.
7. 'If you can't fight, you can't love,' says Sam Keen. Good, clean anger is often to be preferred to sneaky, underhanded ways of getting your own back on your partner for something they don't even know about.
8. The ability to face conflict in a marriage is a sign of its strength, not its weakness. It is usually weak marriages that dare not risk putting their shaky basis to the test.
9. Exposing your inner hurts or resentments to your partner is an act of trust. This may not always be well placed, for to share a need with someone else may

expose your vulnerability and give your partner power over you. But it may be as well to find this out now rather than later.

10. There is such a thing as 'speaking the truth in love'. You can hate an injustice while still loving your partner. By uncovering an issue (say, some unfair expectations about keeping the house clean single-handed when five people are making it dirty) you can enlist the help of the whole family and raise their awareness of how this affects you.
11. By uncovering your feelings about how things are in your marriage and family, you can encourage others to uncover theirs. This may mean a temporarily rocky ride for some of you, but if you keep at it a more rewarding family life can ensue.
12. Conflict is creative when it issues in constructive changes to the satisfaction of both partners in the marriage. Burdens you have borne for years can be off-loaded, not least the guilt you often feel for having such angry feelings in the first place.

Remember: if one partner is unhappy about some aspect of the marriage, the *marriage* is unhappy. Happiness comes from a shared sense of mutual satisfaction; unhappiness is created by one partner nursing an undisclosed grievance.

10. A Case Study

Pat and Brian March have been married for ten years. They have two children, aged 3 and 6. Brian works full-time at a local factory where he is supervisor in charge of the accounts office. Pat works part-time at a chemist's shop. Their six-year-old (Kim) attends the local primary school, while Tammy attends nursery three mornings a week. The March family live in a semi-detached house, a few doors away from Pat's parents.

Pat has been feeling a bit down over the past few weeks. At first she tried to shrug such feelings off as the 'time of the month', but then found she was perpetually tired regardless of her periods.

She began to feel that things were getting on top of her. Their sex life had diminished over the past few months, although Brian had not seemed interested in any case and Pat wondered if he even noticed the lack of intimacy and warmth between them. The children seemed to be even more demanding of late, and Pat's mother was wondering if she could continue to cope with Tammy on the two mornings that she looked after her. There was talk at Brian's firm of redundancies due to a fall-off in orders, and he seemed too preoccupied to notice the drawn look on Pat's face when he got home each evening.

Pat and Brian had experienced bad patches before, especially when Pat had gone through a period of post-natal depression after Tammy was born. The marriage was basically sound and they had always prided themselves on their ability to be frank and open with one another about anything that was bothering them. These past few weeks, however, had seemed different. Both Pat and Brian had gone inside themselves and they were each wrestling with their own agenda.

Things came to a head one evening after Brian had snapped at Pat concerning a telephone message she had forgotten to convey to him. It was not like her to forget such things, but she had too much on her plate to remember everything. That evening she just burst into uncontrollable sobbing after she had put the children to bed.

BRIAN: What on earth's the matter with you?
PAT: (*Sobbing*) I don't know.
BRIAN: You don't know?
PAT: (*Continues sobbing*)
BRIAN: (*Puts down his newspaper, and comes to sit by Pat's side.*) Can you tell me what's wrong?
PAT: Oh, just about everything!
BRIAN: Would you like to talk about it?
PAT: I don't know where to start.
BRIAN: Well, why don't I make a cup of coffee for starters, while you collect your thoughts?
PAT: That sounds like a good idea.

(*Later*)
BRIAN: What went wrong this evening?
PAT: Oh, it's not just this evening; I think it's been brewing for some time.
BRIAN: What's been brewing?
PAT: A general 'fed-upness', I suppose. Life's just got too much for me, and tonight it all poured out.
BRIAN: What in particular is bothering you?
PAT: I don't know how you're going to take this, but it's got a lot to do with feeling taken for granted. My life just seems to consist of getting the children ready for school, you off to work, then there's my job,

running around after the children, housework, shopping, cooking, and Mum doesn't think she can go on looking after Tammy, and that means finding another babysitter – and so it seems to go on and on with no sign of relief.

BRIAN: Why haven't you said anything before?

PAT: Have you seen the look on your face when you come home these days? You seem to be carrying the world on your shoulders! How can I load you with more trouble?

BRIAN: I don't feel you're doing that right now, Pat. I know things are a bit dodgy at work, but we've usually found a way to talk things through when problems arise, haven't we?

PAT: Yes, we have, and I appreciate that, Brian. I think I need to share with you my need for more help, that's all.

BRIAN: Well, can you say what kind of help you need?

PAT: Well, to start with, I'd like you to take a bit more responsibility for the children. For instance, could you drop Tammy off on your way to work now and then? That would be one less thing for me to think about in the morning.

BRIAN: I don't see any problem about that. Provided she's ready of course when I leave.

PAT: But that's just making me responsible again, isn't it? It would be nice if you could help out with getting the kids ready, instead of leaving them *and* breakfast, *and* washing up, all to me.

BRIAN: You seem angry with me.

PAT: Well, to be truthful I am. I haven't recognized it until now, but I do feel you just don't notice me struggling every morning. They're your kids too, you know. It's all very well to spend time playing with them, but it's me that's left to put them to bed each night. Why don't you do it now and then?

BRIAN: I've never thought about it, I suppose. You've always seemed to take charge of the kids, so I've not thought of interfering with your way of doing things.

PAT: Well, the way I feel right now, any interference as you call it would be very welcome. (*She smiles.*)

BRIAN: OK. I hear what you say. Perhaps we can work out the nitty-gritty tomorrow, but I'll need to know where you keep the kids' things.

PAT: It'd be a pleasure! I'm not passing the buck, Brian, but I am asking for a bit more consideration from you, so that life can run more smoothly in the future.

BRIAN: I'm sorry, love, that I've missed this. It's so easy to get into a routine about the running of the house that in the end I suppose we both end up by taking things for granted.

PAT: That's what I've been feeling for some time now, but I've just bottled it all up until tonight when it all came pouring out.

BRIAN: While we're on the subject of bottling things up, it's not just you that's been doing it; I've been meaning to talk to you about our sex life, but I guess I've been avoiding it. I do miss the closeness we used to enjoy, but frankly you've not appeared to be interested lately.

PAT: You're right. I just haven't had the energy or the interest for some time.

BRIAN: You haven't gone off me, have you?

PAT: Of course not. Give me a hug, you old softy!

Pat and Brian may be thought of as representing a positive model (not an *ideal* one) of what a renegotiating process might look like in practice. Given the basic stability of their marriage relationship, and their undoubted ability to be able to sit down and *listen* to one another, the above situation illustrates several of the points made in chapter 9, and outlined on p. 76.

1. Pat was not asking Brian for anything that was impossible. Helping with the kids may mean a new morning

routine but there is nothing in Pat's request that was intrinsically beyond Brian's capacity. This showed, to both of them, there was sufficient flexibility in the relationship to make an important improvement in lessening the sense of chaos in the March family's 'rush hour'.

2. By spending the evening levelling with one another, they put down an important 'marker' for the improvement of their communication which is shown to be needed in the present situation.
3. Pat was challenging the assumption that the children were 'women's work'.
4. The issue concerning the children gave to both Pat and Brian the opportunity to re-evaluate the distribution of labour in the family.
5. Eventually, the resentments that Pat had been 'bottling up' broke through her defences and demanded that the issues underneath be given attention.
6. Although Pat may have felt 'out of control' once she broke down, both she and Brian could see that the marriage was not out of control. Some adjustments to their sex life were needed, as Brian was brave enough to mention. Once this was recognized and the issue placed on the marital agenda, their sense of being in control was reinforced.
7. This interaction reveals Brian's hidden assumptions that had been one of the precipitating causes of this encounter.
8. The process of renegotiation provided both of them with an opportunity to open up areas of their feelings which perhaps the very busyness of life might otherwise have allowed to go by without further examination.
9. This encounter illustrates how intimacy can actually be increased by honest confrontation of issues which are proving an obstacle to their future enjoyment of one another.
10. Any further distancing of Pat and Brian at an intimate

> level was curtailed by this open conversation. It prevented the erosion of love by a joint willingness to remove some of the obstacles which otherwise may have stood in the way of their future happiness.

As much as some of us may want to avoid conflict at all costs, the case of Pat and Brian provide a positive model of 'creative conflict' at work. This encounter, of course, is simply by way of illustration. Each couple will have their own unique way of communicating, their own familiar way of expressing themselves, not least in body-language, that makes any model merely illustrative. Yet it may come as a surprise to find how 'normal' such a conversation can be. Naturally, it begs several questions, not least Brian's willingness to listen and to respond creatively to what Pat is saying. I realize that some husbands would simply close the door and go to the pub. (Such avoidance would, of course, need confronting.) Yet in 'good enough' marriages there is usually enough goodwill to want to remove any barriers that stand in the way of increased intimacy, love and respect.

Above all, there was no destructive blaming going on between Pat and Brian. It was Brian's attitude that was confronted by Pat and which she disliked, rather than Brian as a person. This is a crucial distinction. When Brian agreed to drop Tammy off to Pat's mother, he was assuming she would appear already dressed and ready to go. That doesn't happen by magic, and Pat was brave enough to confront Brian about that. Pat talked about responsibility, and that proved a more constructive way of reaching Brian than blaming him. Pat also models a creative way of using anger to energize her self-protection. Her boundaries were collapsing all around her, and in this encounter she was fighting for the relationship just as much as for herself. Here is a good model for the constructive use of anger to defend her collapsing boundaries – and it seems to have worked. When this happens we are encouraged to make use of it in all situations where we feel invaded, put upon, or simply taken for granted. Solid marriages need not fear honest expressions of anger. Pat and Brian's marriage would have been fortified by this interaction, and so the foundation for further periods of renegotiation in the future would be strengthened.

Brian, encouraged by Pat's honest admission of 'bottling up' her feelings, was able to broach the subject of their sex life but in a very understanding yet firm way. He was not making demands; he did not counter-attack. He did not sulk or go silent. He admitted having avoided the subject, and it is interesting to note the part their mutual tiredness and anxiety, in terms of non-verbal body-language, played in the run-up to this conversation. Brian had the courage to ask for reassurance that Pat had not 'gone off' him – which opened up his own need and vulnerability – and received a warm reassurance that this was not so. Even in her distress, Pat found it possible to reaffirm her appreciation of their ability to be open and honest with one another about things that worried them, and to respond to his needs. We may perhaps be witnessing in this encounter a New Man in the making, and the renewed enjoyment of an obviously important relationship.

This encounter also illustrates another important issue. As Brian was able to *lean into* the feelings of his wife and make a practical response to them, he also broke out of his own defensive behaviour of not speaking about their sex life. As he moved towards his wife's feelings, he moved closer to his own. This is often found to be the case when couples move closer to one another. Personal growth often accompanies greater experiences of intimacy as we learn to trust one another more with our own inner worlds.

The question of increased intimacy demands our further examination.

11. Enriching Marital Intimacy

Understanding intimacy

'Intimacy' needs liberating.

For as long as I can remember, 'intimacy' has been equated with 'sex'. 'Being intimate' meant 'having sex'. An 'intimate friendship' was but a euphemism for 'carnal knowledge'. *The Concise Oxford Dictionary of Current English* defines intimacy as; 'State of being intimate; (euphem.) sexual intercourse.' I share the sentiments of Tom Oden when he writes, 'I regret that so many modern men and women have become trapped in the twisted assumption that intimacy is reducible to coital scoring.'[35] So, as with an old oil painting, perhaps we need to take the word 'intimacy' off the wall and give it a good clean, to see what its original meaning looked like.

The Latin word *intimus* means 'inner' or 'innermost'. Tom Oden provides a useful guide to understanding the meaning of intimacy:

> Influenced by this nuance of innermost, our English word *intimate* points to a particular kind of knowing, a knowledge of the core of something, an understanding of the inmost parts, that which is indicative of one's deepest nature and marked by close physical, mental, or social association. The biblical word for sexual closeness is this sort of knowing: 'Adam knew Eve'. When I am in touch with the *intimum* of another, I know that which is ordinarily hidden from public view yet revealed in the closeness and vulnerability of the relationship. When I

> am aware that someone else is in touch with my own *intimum* I know I have been reached at the deeper levels of my consciousness.[36]

In order to widen still further our understanding of intimacy, and to clean off the ancient accretions, I quote from the helpful analysis of Howard and Charlotte Clinebell.[37] They list twelve facets or levels of intimacy which characterize deep and close relationships, thus expanding our understanding of the potentially wide range of such relationships:

1.	Sexual intimacy	(erotic or orgasmic closeness).
2.	Emotional intimacy	(being tuned to each other's wavelength).
3.	Intellectual intimacy	(closeness in the world of ideas).
4.	Aesthetic intimacy	(sharing experience of beauty).
5.	Creative intimacy	(sharing in acts of creating together).
6.	Recreational intimacy	(relating in experiences of fun and play).
7.	Work intimacy	(the closeness of sharing common tasks).
8.	Crisis intimacy	(closeness in coping with problems and pain).
9.	Conflict intimacy	(facing and struggling with differences).
10.	Commitment intimacy	(mutuality derived from common self-investment).
11.	Spiritual intimacy	(the we-ness in sharing ultimate concerns).
12.	Communication intimacy	(the source of all types of true intimacy).

Implications for married couples

A number of conclusions may be drawn from this expanded description of intimate relationships:

- Sexual intimacy is only one of many ways of relating to people intimately.
- Intimate relationships are therefore viable – and perhaps desirable – far beyond the narrow confines of marriage.
- Intimate relationships are capable of being expressed by people of the same sex without them being regarded as in any way homosexual.
- We may know other people intimately without necessarily placing our marriage at risk.
- There are a multiplicity of areas of our partner's life that we may never have thought of as potential resources for the enrichment of our marriage.
- To relate to our partner only at the sexual level of intimacy detracts from the full range of a truly intimate marriage.
- To use sex as the sole medium of expressing and receiving intimacy is to place upon it an unbearable burden and unrealistic expectations.
- Intimate relationships are not necessarily the same as *genital* relationships.
- A wide range of intimate relationships increases the flow of resources into our lives, and decreases any unrealistic or neurotic dependence upon our partner to meet all our needs.
- We are all capable of relating to other people in a wide variety of ways, and of sharing with our partner the whole of our self-understanding.

These ideas are light years away from the traditionally narrow (and deficient) understanding of intimacy, and perhaps help us to see the importance of revising both our understanding of intimacy and our expectations from an intimate relationship. You are also, perhaps, increasing your own awareness of the vast potential that exists within your marriage for a deeper, and more rewarding, intimate relationship.

Checking up on your marital intimacy

To enable you to take such awareness a step further in the process of enriching your marriage, I reproduce (by their kind permission) the Clinebells' 'Marital Intimacy Check-up' as a way of assessing for yourselves the present state of each of these areas of intimacy and to discover in what ways you would both like to see improvements.

One way would be for you and your partner to discuss this together and then *tick the appropriate blanks*. The purpose of the exercise I will explain later. Just for now, be as honest as you can as you apply it to your marriage.

MARITAL INTIMACY CHECK-UP

Facet of intimacy (fuller details are on p. 88)	*Both desire improvement*	*Wife desires improvement*	*Husband desires improvement*	*Both satisfied*
1. Sexual:	—	—	—	—
2. Emotional:	—	—	—	—
3. Intellectual:	—	—	—	—
4. Aesthetic:	—	—	—	—
5. Creative:	—	—	—	—
6. Recreational:	—	—	—	—
7. Work:	—	—	—	—
8. Crisis:	—	—	—	—
9. Conflict:	—	—	—	—
10. Commitment:	—	—	—	—
11. Spiritual:	—	—	—	—
12. Communication:	—	—	—	—

Having completed this exercise, you now have the makings of a 'plan of action' towards enriching your marriage. It is totally unique to your marriage, and concerns only you and your partner. How you use the information this exercise has disclosed is, of course, entirely a matter for you to choose. But here are a few suggestions you may like to consider together by way of implementing desirable change.

Step 1: Notice the ticks in the column headed 'Both satisfied'. These will indicate the *strengths* in your marriage, and the areas that are going well.

Step 2: Notice the areas you have ticked where both are desiring improvement to a facet of your intimacy as these indicate areas of *mutual concern*. You may need to discuss which of these agreed concerns should be given priority, and find ways of implementing the improvements you are seeking.

Step 3: The remaining two columns represent your own individual concerns about your marriage. You have uncovered *desired improvements* each of you would like to make to your relationship with your partner. These desired improvements, if allowed to go unattended, represent potential flash-points in the marriage.

The case of Henry and Ava

When Henry and Ava completed their Marital Intimacy Check-up, this is what they found. Their plan looked like this:

MARITAL INTIMACY CHECK-UP

Facet of intimacy	*Both desire improvement*	*Wife desires improvement*	*Husband desires improvement*	*Both satisfied*
1. Sexual:	—	—	•	—
2. Emotional:	•	—	—	—
3. Intellectual:	—	—	—	•
4. Aesthetic:	—	—	—	•
5. Creative:	—	•	—	—
6. Recreational:	—	—	•	—
7. Work:	—	•	—	—
8. Crisis:	—	•	—	—
9. Conflict:	•	—	—	—
10. Commitment:	—	—	—	•
11. Spiritual:	—	—	•	—
12. Communication:	—	•	—	—

First of all, what are the *strengths* of this relationship? Henry and Ava see these in the intellectual and aesthetic areas of their intimacy. In fact, both of them are avid readers and enjoy intellectual pursuits; their aesthetic interests include visits to art galleries, travel and their support of the National Trust. There is also the strength of their commitment to one another. Their marriage is soundly based and they enjoy one another's company.

Secondly, they both perceive *weaknesses* in the areas of emotional expression and coping with conflict. Of course, these two areas are closely related. Conflict often requires the expression of strong emotions. They are stronger in their intellectual apprehension and understanding of life than in its emotional expression, and they are both desiring improvement in these important areas. It is in fact an additional strength that they can identify these weaker areas of their marriage, and together create a plan of action in order to deal with them. For instance, they may discuss these with friends whom they trust, or they could be the subject of a short period of marriage counselling. Either way, Henry and Ava are agreed that they need some help in coping with conflict and emotional expression.

Thirdly, Henry's perceived needs lie in the areas of sexual, recreational and spiritual intimacy. Because their marriage is broadly based on many levels of intimacy, Henry does not see sex as the be-all and end-all of their marriage. He enjoys Ava in many ways, but he would like to see an improvement in their sex life (see next chapter). In their marital check-up this came out quite clearly to both of them, Ava appearing to be happy with the *status quo*, while Henry was not. Of the three areas in which Henry would like to see improvement, he is in little doubt that their sex life is by far the most important. By identifying his need, he can place it on the 'plan of action', the marital agenda to which Henry and Ava are addressing themselves. But for this check-up process, Henry would have kept his dissatisfaction to himself; but now he feels able to express it openly, and share with Ava his need for greater sexual satisfaction. In the light of this need, the other two areas seem rather insignificant and he would not have bothered to raise them had they not been on the check-list. However, he would like to see improvement in Ava's support of his recreational and church activities. He knows that church is not really Ava's scene, but he often feels that the whole issue of religion and ultimate values in life gets pushed off their marital agenda.

Fourthly, Ava would like to see improvements in four areas of their marriage: creativity, work, crisis and communication. For Ava, the latter is by far the most important. Ava feels that sometimes their marriage survives on its silences rather than verbal expression. Because of the deep understanding they have of one another, Henry feels that words are not always needed to convey meanings and feelings. But Ava needs a more open communication between them, and to hear Henry express verbally how he feels about himself, his work and life in general. Henry can now begin to process Ava's need for improvement in this area, and in the others she has identified on her check-list. Ava, for instance, would like to see Henry share with her in some of the common household tasks. There has been an assumption of late that the home is the exclusive responsibility of Ava, and she gets tired of reminding Henry of the jobs that need doing which she feels are beyond her. When crises hit the wider family, Henry is usually conspicuous by his absence. He finds it hard to cope with emotional problems, hence their shared awareness that they both need help with this area.

Perhaps this couple illustrate the usefulness of this kind of occasional check-up, especially since it can throw up hidden and subconscious grievances or desires which otherwise might go unnoticed. It can reveal hidden agendas which experience teaches us comprise the raw material for major problems in human relationships, especially within marriage. Given the existing strengths of Henry and Ava's marriage there is every likelihood that, in their own way and in their own time, they will address themselves to practical ways of meeting their individual and corporate needs for the enrichment of their marriage.

Hidden strengths and weaknesses

I believe that Howard Clinebell is correct when he says,

> In most marriages there's a hidden marriage waiting to be discovered and liberated. This latent marriage is a better marriage – more fulfilling, more intimate, more alive – than the here-and-now relationship. The latent marriage may be well hidden – buried under many layers of anger, mutual neglect, and hurting . . . It's the unlived life in our marriages that make them so vulnerable in crises we otherwise could take in our stride.[38]

Of course, this 'hidden marriage' is quite different in nature to the 'unconscious marriage' referred to earlier (p. 40). Strategies such as the marital check-up inventory we have just discussed may therefore be seen as a vital diagnostic technique that can uncover the hidden strengths and weaknesses in our marriage. This may seem like hard work, but wherever did we get the idea that good and rewarding marriages just happen? Especially is such work needed in what may be called the 'mid-term marriage'.

The mid-term marriage

Once the relationship has been going for some while, say seven years or more, it is seldom appreciated that the partners are seven years older, that times have changed, and sometimes they have changed too. What you looked for at the outset of your marriage may not be what you are looking for now. What you did not need seven years ago, you may have a desperate need for in the here-and-now. As much as we would like it to be otherwise, life does not stand still – and neither do we.

It is precisely at this point that many married couples

feel themselves to be stuck. There is no magical importance attaching to a seven-year marriage, although there is something in the so-called 'seven-year itch'. Life often seems to go in seven-year cycles: the ages of 7, 14 and 21 are usually important turning points in our lives. When Jan and I celebrated our seventh wedding anniversary, we both felt that we had come to a watershed in our relationship that neither of us were aware of on our fifth anniversary. Of course, it could have been that we were aware of the cultural warning about the 'seven-year itch' once we had reached it; after all, there is no tradition of a 'five-year itch'. Some of these old sayings are grounded in some basis of fact, and both Jan and I were glad that it provided us with a good opportunity for a review of our marriage.

It is significant to note that among people getting divorced, 'Overall, the median length of marriage is about 10 years, with marriages where the divorce is granted to the husband lasting a little longer than those granted to the wife.'[39] In *Social Trends 20* (1990), the highest rate of divorces (28 per cent) is found among those whose marriages have lasted between 5 and 9 years. In the light of this information many couples are coming to appreciate that, somewhere along their journey together, it is good to stop and assess where the marriage is going, and how they can be in control of that process. This is where marriage enrichment programmes provide a most useful focus for such assessment. It allows us to discover our 'hidden marriage'.

A mid-term marriage review may be useful when any major change affects the marital relationship. Such major changes would include:

1. Moving house.
2. Children starting, or leaving, school.
3. Redundancy.
4. Change to part-time work.
5. Starting a new job.
6. Retirement.

7. Illness of a partner.
8. Changes in income and expenditure.
9. Promotion.
10. Wife going out to work or giving up job.
11. A death in the family.
12. Children leaving home.
13. Marital separation.
14. Parents or in-laws moving in (or out).
15. An important wedding anniversary.

For instance, the 'empty-nest' syndrome, when all the children have left home, is one of these major changes. In this case, a massive realignment is called for, since the marriage can no longer enjoy the focus of the children to determine its future shape as in the past. This can be a crisis-point for many couples, especially for those who have traditionally used the children as a 'buffer' to closer intimacy. It is now a case of Jack and Jill alone each day, and this opens up an opportunity for a new potential of life free from the parental roles that have been a major preoccupation for the past twenty years or more. At the same time, it can feel very threatening to be the focus of your partner day in and day out.

The hidden marriage can come into its own at this point in the relationship. This particular change in situation, that proves so threatening to some, may come as a life-saver to others. It can provide the leisure to concentrate upon the needs of the two people in the marriage, and together plan for their future. While the outcome must always remain, to some extent at least, uncertain, what is certain is that enrichment is not just going to happen automatically. It will take concentration, determination, courage and a good deal of honesty to ensure that 'the best is yet to be'.

To end this brief look at enriching marital intimacy, there is one subject that needs attention, for it challenges some of the assumptions that I have been making so far. Supposing that opening ourselves up to our partners at very deep levels proves too threatening for words? What about those people who, for various reasons, have come to dread closeness whether emotional, physical or sexual?

Dread of intimacy

It may not be surprising to note that some people do not enjoy closeness, either physical or emotional. Robin Skynner points out that 'responsibility for ensuring closeness is usually taken on by the female, that for distance, by the male'. He adds a useful nautical analogy, '. . . she is in charge of the grappling-irons and tries to make him stay home more, while he is in charge of the fenders, complains about her possessiveness and finds excuses to be out doing other things'.[40] Each of us can recall people we know who seem to keep themselves to themselves, even within a stable marriage.

Not everyone appreciates being touched; for some, intimacy is something that they have come to dread, and thus to avoid at all costs. In my enthusiasm – or in *my* unrecognized need for touch – I have unthinkingly broken through the boundaries of other people, and sometimes they have had the honesty to tell me so. My own assumption is that closeness, physical and emotional, is a 'good thing', and I have not always been aware of those around me to whom it has posed a threat of gigantic proportions. I remember my friend Jackie who was about to get the Gough bear-hug treatment retreating from me with her hands held up to ward me off, saying, 'Too close, Tony!' Thankfully, in the trust and openness of our friendship she could share that with me, in time for me to draw back and honour her boundaries. I do not always get distance right, but I know that I am wrong to project my own attitudes toward intimacy upon others, *without checking it out.* Hence these final paragraphs.

A dread of intimacy usually has its origins in our past experience of life. It can come from two opposite directions: from having been swamped and engulfed as children by adults, or by being physically and emotionally neglected as children. Both are extremes. Too much closeness, and we have our boundaries invaded, and in very early life this can wreak havoc with our sense of separateness and ultimately to our sense of identity. Not enough intimacy, and we can imagine ourselves to be dirty, unclean, untouchable, and we learn to bury our need for physical contact beneath a pleasing exterior.

Dr Frank Lake, basing his understanding on the researches of the Russian physiologist, Ivan Pavlov (1849–1936), used to speak of the phenomenon known in psychology as 'trans-marginal stress'. Briefly, it is a bit like metal fatigue: when stressed to its limits, it breaks. In a similar way, children can be stressed to their limits of tolerance and, like Pavlov's experiments on his dogs, what was once longed for with life-preserving intensity is now rejected with equal force. Children then present as stand-offish, not liking to be touched, while all the while (inside) *desperately wanting* to be physically affirmed. What prevents them from acting on this inner longing is the refusal – amounting sometimes to absolute panic – to place themselves in the situation where they had to rely on other people to meet their needs. To open themselves up to touch would open up their painful experiences of how it felt to want physical contact and not to receive it. It is, of course, a paradox, but it is one way of understanding how some people have come to dread intimacy and being known in their innermost reality.

This latter point is also important in our understanding of those marriages where a partner appears to be distant and does not want their space invaded. Many people I have spoken to in the course of their therapy reveal to me their dread of being known by anyone else. They fear that, if anyone really knew them (in an intimate way) they would be rejected. One woman who felt herself to be totally bad inside, dreaded having to share that bit of herself should she form a deep and intimate relationship. Many people can understand how she felt. With such a low sense of self-esteem, and a very depleted self-image, she felt sure that no one could possibly love her, once they discovered 'what I'm really like inside'. The writer John Powell tells of the preparations for his book *Why Am I Afraid to Tell You Who I Am?* 'Do you want me to answer that question?' a friend replied. He went on, 'I am afraid to tell you who I am, because, if I tell you who I am, you may not like who I am, and it's all that I have.'[41] I have met hundreds of people who would have given that reply, as they confront their own dread of intimacy.

Here is another part of the hidden marriage referred to above. It represents that part of us that has still to be revealed to our partner. Those who continue to conceal their inmost being have one advantage; they do not have to risk rejection of those parts of themselves that they cannot cope with and imagine that their partner would not be able to cope with either. But against that advantage is one big disadvantage; how can they *know* they are loved, if they only present to their partner those bits they think they can cope with? When they hear their partner express their love for them, they will have to make constant discounts in their head. For in truth, love expressed needs to become love received. And if there are parts of ourselves that we hate and find disgusting, we will be unable to allow them to be the recipients of our partner's love. We will find ourselves playing games in our head: 'If you *really* knew me you would not be saying that!' Thus, rejecting parts of ourself we will imagine that our partner would reject them also; not loving ourselves wholly, we cannot allow anyone else to love us totally.

Marital therapists spend most of their professional lives dealing with the results of this kind of reactive behaviour. My experience is that it is a major cause of marriage break-down. Of course, some couples learn to live with it; physical touch, expressions of warmth and emotion and, of course, sex are all off the marital menu. Rather than leave the marriage some learn to adjust to their emotionally sterile situation. They sublimate their sexual frustration by gardening, excessive jogging or other physical and intellectual distractions. But by far the majority find their emotional isolation more than they can bear; often in sheer desperation, and against their own code of ethics, they find a partner outside the marriage who is open to their love and warmth, and to whom – to their utter amazement – they find themselves to be totally lovable, even desirable. The rest, as they say, is statistics!

As Sheldon Kopp says, 'Revealing myself to others always involves taking a chance. But hiding out can be just as risky. If no one knows me, who can love me?'[42]

12. Enriching Sexual Intimacy

The sexual revolution

During the past thirty years or so, a sexual revolution has taken place, especially in the Western world, that has drastically changed social attitudes concerning sex. This has been brought about partly (but not wholly) by the women's movement. It now takes an effort of imagination to get inside the sexual world-view of, say, the 1950s even for those of us who were around at that time. Anyone reading this who is under forty has only history to rely on and the stories that their parents have to tell – if they dare! Clearly, this revolution has had an important and vital impact upon modern marriage, and those getting married in the 1990s will have a totally different outlook and set of expectations than those of their parents.

Like other revolutions, the sexual one contained a combination of the good, the bad and the ugly, depending on your viewpoint. Greater freedom of sexual expression, the increasing expectations of women for a full and satisfying sex life, the availability of sex manuals and 'marital aids', soft- and hard-porn literature and videos, and a slightly less self-consciousness about the subject of sex, are some of the major claims of the sexual revolution. Some of the less welcome results, for many people, are an increase in promiscuity (but by what yardstick is this to be compared, say, with the Victorian era?), an increase in sexually-transmitted diseases including the current epidemic of AIDS, an increase in children born out of wedlock with a consequential rise in the number of single-parent families and their cost to the taxpayer of billions of pounds in state-funded aid. One thing is for sure: sex is now out of the prissy, Victorian cupboard and there is no putting it back. Young children now receive quite explicit sex education in state schools, including the use and value of contraceptive methods. 'Safe sex' is the subject of a widespread advertising campaign, and condoms have even appeared on TV commercials.

Within the context of this wider revolution, marriage has been drastically affected by the change of cultural attitudes and wider choices available to most couples today. I have already drawn attention to the dangers of placing upon a satisfying sex life the entire weight of marital harmony. However, it is still true to say that, not forgetting the importance of good communication, there are perhaps more potential problems in the area of erotic fulfilment than in any other area of a marriage. It would be dodging the issue not to address these at this point.

Sex in the early years of marriage

In contrast to our experiences of 'brotherly love' (love among equals) and 'motherly love' (love for the helpless), Erich Fromm distinguishes 'erotic love' as 'the craving for complete fusion'.[43] In the human experience that we describe as 'falling in love', two people, possibly strangers, are aware of the sudden collapse of their psychological boundaries. As Fromm writes,

> If two people who have been strangers, as all of us are, suddenly let the wall between them break down, and feel close, feel one, this moment of oneness is one of the most exhilarating, most exciting experiences in life. It is all the more wonderful and miraculous for persons who have been shut off, isolated, without love. This miracle of sudden intimacy is often facilitated if it is

> combined with, or initiated by, sexual attraction and consummation. However, this type of love is by its very nature not lasting . . . Yet, in the beginning they do not know all this: in fact, they take the intensity of the infatuation, this being crazy about each other, for proof of the intensity of their love, while it may only prove the degree of their preceding loneliness.[44]

The experience of *falling in love* is very often succeeded by the state of *being in love*, a deeper, less ephemeral condition. Other parts of the lover are being explored and appreciated and a wider base for a future relationship established. We reveal more of ourselves within the trust and depths of our intimacy, and the erotic pleasure given and received takes its place among other facets of human intimacy, such as those we looked at in chapter 11.

It is commonly assumed that, in these early years of the relationship, there will be no problems concerning sexual performance or sexual enjoyment. Such an assumption is reinforced by a more open cultural stance than ever before. Yet, to the surprise of many people, there is an incredible amount of ignorance and naivity among some young people, and what they will boast of among their friends ('sexier than thou!') becomes a different story in the fumblings and self-consciousness of their early experiences of sexual intercourse. In perhaps the majority of marriages (reliable evidence is hard to find) most of the wrinkles are ironed out in the first few months as the two people have time and energy to spend with each other. Eventually, sexual preferences are explored, the parameters of our partner's range of responses are understood and accepted, and an understanding is reached that will enable the couple to go on enjoying a full sex life for many years to come.

Honesty, laced with a little humour, usually sees most couples through these early years of sexual enjoyment. These days, more than ever before, younger couples experiencing any kind of sexual dysfunction are likely to visit their doctor, a marriage guidance (RELATE) counsellor or sex therapist. These resources are now commonplace and are largely free from association with social incompetence or shame. In a TV programme in which I took part, a couple appeared who had overcome the problem of premature ejaculation through a short course of sex therapy. Their sex therapist (Sue Wood) spoke of the greater readiness on the part of married couples to avail themselves of such therapy today, in contrast to the guilt, shame and denial in former years.

However, there are further problems that may arise later on in some marriages.

Sex in the mid-term marriage

Sexual boredom is the number-one enemy in most mid-term marriages. The excitement of the chase and discovery of our lover no longer applies. Most of the range of sexual expressions have been run through, at least those of which we are physically capable! We know our partners so well, and this period is often known as the 'settling down' period. Life becomes predictable. The family routine largely governs the way we live, and by our early thirties our life pattern is usually laid down in concrete. This is not to say that the marriage does not have its pleasures. It's just that, especially where there are children, our life seems to be running away from us; we can feel that our life is out of control.

Anything that can affect our emotional or physical well-being is bound to have an effect on our sex life. Anxiety, depression, sickness, concern over finances, our sense of ageing, all these easily affect the way we feel about ourselves and divert energy into a survival mode and away from sexual expression. Indeed, in the majority of cases, when sexual dysfunction is presented to our doctor it is not due to any organic, physical deficiency in us. It is often found to be the result of other factors like anxiety or depression. Unspoken anger or hidden resentment also figure very highly among the emotional causes of libidinal loss. These factors are more likely to affect the mid-term period of a marriage than earlier on in the relationship.

As this book is addressed directly to those marriages that are basically stable and sound, and where life between you and your partner is certainly 'good enough', how can your sex life be enriched? What I propose is to offer you another self-help awareness exercise in which you and your partner can assess how far you wish to improve your sexual enjoyment, and ways of implementing it.

Love-life satisfaction

The awareness exercise starting on p. 106 is designed to help you discover your present levels of satisfaction. Remember, it is offered as a simple *awareness* exercise, not as a prelude to World War III! It affords both you and your partner an opportunity to hear and understand some of the things you have been feeling but have never shared. Or, having shared them often, your partner has never listened enough to make any changes to meet your needs. One of the important uses of such exercises is that it can increase the range and depth of communication between you.

First read the questionnaire through. Then go through it again, placing a tick in the column you feel comes nearest to how you experience each facet of your mutual love-making. OK means you are satisfied; NOT OK means you are not satisfied. Keep in mind that you are trying to discover the extent to which you are satisfied with your love-life, not how good you are at giving these various expressions of your love (your partner will help you discover that).

If you continue right through this awareness exercise you will end up with your own personal satisfaction guide regarding your love-life: foreplay, intercourse and post-coital activities (if any).

LOVE-LIFE SATISFACTION QUESTIONNAIRE (H = husband, W = wife)	OK		NOT OK	
	H	W	H	W
PART 1: Expressions of loving and caring				
1. Everyday expressions of tenderness and affection (not as a prelude to intercourse)	—	—	—	—
2. Receiving consideration and understanding on a day-to-day basis	—	—	—	—
3. Allowing time for you to share mutual concerns	—	—	—	—
4. Attentive listening to you on a regular basis – not just in crisis	—	—	—	—
5. Thoughtfulness in everyday expressions of care for you by your partner	—	—	—	—
6. Given surprises other than on special anniversaries during the year	—	—	—	—
7. Expressions of concern for you without having to be requested	—	—	—	—
8. Offering you help and support with your work	—	—	—	—
9. Gentle and affectionate physical contact and touching	—	—	—	—
10. Affirmation of love by kissing and cuddling	—	—	—	—
PART 2: Prelude to intercourse (Foreplay)				
How satisfied are you with:				
1. Creation of a romantic atmosphere, candles, warmth, soft lighting, music	—	—	—	—

	OK		NOT OK	
	H	W	H	W
2. Hygenic preparation, bathing, shower, use of perfumes or oils	—	—	—	—
3. Gentle and loving stimulation of sensitive areas of your body	—	—	—	—
4. Responsiveness by your partner to your erogenous zones	—	—	—	—
5. Timing of the build-up towards intercourse	—	—	—	—
6. Gentle caressing of your genitals	—	—	—	—
7. Strong caressing of your genitals	—	—	—	—
8. Flexibility of your partner to respond to expressed needs	—	—	—	—
9. The use of oral sex during this foreplay period	—	—	—	—
10. The timing of penetration	—	—	—	—
11. Undressing – or being undressed by – your partner	—	—	—	—
12. The level of activity of your partner (body movements, responses, closeness)	—	—	—	—
PART 3: Intercourse				
Try to assess your present degree of satisfaction with:				
1. Frequency of intercourse	—	—	—	—
2. Time spent on foreplay and intercourse	—	—	—	—
3. Your partner's concern for your feelings during intercourse	—	—	—	—
4. Your normal physical position during intercourse	—	—	—	—
5. Variety of positions attempted so far	—	—	—	—

	OK		NOT OK	
	H	W	H	W
6. Responsiveness by your partner to what feels right for you	—	—	—	—
7. More prolonged intercourse	—	—	—	—
8. Oral sex	—	—	—	—
9. Achieving a satisfactory climax	—	—	—	—
10. Use of books, pictures and/or 'marital aids' (e.g. vibrator)	—	—	—	—
11. Present quality of communication about sexual intercourse	—	—	—	—
12. In general, is sex OK or Not OK	—	—	—	—
PART 4: After Intercourse				
Specific occasions may vary, but *in general* express your degree of satisfaction with:				
1. Expressions of love, tenderness, affection after intercourse	—	—	—	—
2. Time spent together after intercourse	—	—	—	—
3. Your sleep needs after intercourse	—	—	—	—
4. Partner's co-operation in the 'mopping up' period	—	—	—	—
5. The variety of post-coital activities	—	—	—	—

As well as having compiled your own personal satisfaction guide, you will also discover two other important features of your marriage. First, you will discover, by the number of agreed 'OKs', the areas where you are both, in general, satisfied with things as they are. These are the strengths of your sexual relations and need to be acknowledged as such. They are also valuable building blocks upon which further happiness and contentment can be built. Secondly, you will identify the 'Not OK' areas where in general you are not satisfied and in which you would like to see some improvement.

You may find that you aren't going to reverse all the sexual habits of a long marriage overnight. Rather, choose from your own list of 'Not OKs' the items that seem most important to you, rather than hit your partner over the head with the whole lot at once. Work through them one at a time: 'This time I'd like you to . . .' 'How about trying . . . ?' 'I'd really love it if you would . . .' This is another example of the renegotiation process referred to on page 76 and can lead to an enhancement of your enjoyment of sex with your partner. It's OK to say how you feel about the way your partner treats you in bed – unless you are among those who fall into the trap of suffering in silence because 'I wouldn't like to upset him/her'.

Learning to vocalize your needs

Sometimes it is just not possible to get what you want without the risk of upsetting your partner. You have a choice: you remain dissatisfied, and thus create a dangerous vacuum of need which may not stay empty for ever, or you run the risk of your partner getting hurt. Many couples in their mid-years feel like this, and they express their quandary in many ways. Perhaps the majority go on feeling hurt themselves rather than run the risk of vocalizing their needs and possibly hurting their partners. Traditionally it has been women who feel like this most of the time.

There seems to be a need in the male gene to feel successful in bed. The locker-room stories are an example of both 'one-upmanship' and 'hornier-than-thou' communication. Often they represent a flight into fantasy. No one hears men boasting of their impotence, or premature ejaculation! I doubt if any man would tell his friends that his wife never has an orgasm – the shame would be too great for words. (Of course, if only such men would leave their partner to determine the level of their own orgasmic experience, the pressure – and perhaps subsequent feelings of guilt – would be taken off both of them.)

If we were to overhear these men's wives talking, perhaps a different story would emerge. 'Fake' orgasms may be more the order of the day than their husbands could ever cope with. (Any woman whose husband does not believe in 'fake orgasms', should take him to see the film based on Nora Ephron's book, *When Harry met Sally*; it could be an education!)

But to return to the problem of how to share your dissatisfaction with your partner. The principle I would offer to you is this: you are not actually responsible for the feelings of your partner. Of course you love them, and do not want to hurt them in any way. But do you really believe that by *not* telling them how you feel you are not hurting them? You are withholding truth and honesty from your relationship – and that can only do long-term harm to your marriage. You may actually be deceiving them, lying to them in fact, and experience tells us that this can prove far more hurtful than the subject you are withholding. Frankly, it is not always possible to convey our feelings to another person without them feeling hurt; we may not intend to hurt them, but how else do we maintain our honesty and integrity with them? By allowing your partner to be responsible for their feelings, and you for your own, you can convey your need for improvement in your sex life without necessarily feeling guilty or taking responsibility for how they feel about what you have said.

When we withhold our feelings from our partner there is the added danger that instead of conveying them openly we will convey them by hidden, underhanded means. Take for instance the use of sarcasm. As we noticed earlier (p. 60) this is a hidden form of anger. So, instead of asking our partner to slow down during intercourse, we may instead snipe at him and ask, 'Have you got a train to catch?' The feelings of dissatisfaction have been conveyed effectively, but in an indirect way. By using sarcasm, we wound our partner with biting ridicule, which is often much more hurtful than the truth. Sarcasm diminishes our partner by attacking his pride and sense of well-being; by honestly saying that we want him to slow down, we give him a chance to adjust his speed, and increase the mutual sense of enjoyment. That way, both are fulfilled.

Sarcasm, when it is used as a regular means of indirect communication, slowly poisons a relationship. Behind the sarcasm is usually a great deal of unhappiness, resentment or pain. If you can find more direct ways of expressing this to your partner, you may find that he is not quite as fragile as you make him out to be. Fantasies such as, 'He'd fall apart if I told him that,' simply need checking out. In the case of male potency, it may hurt his pride but he may come to thank you for that in due course.

Similarly, with female unresponsiveness. If a woman is not actively enjoying her sex life, and is withholding from her husband, do you really think she does not know it? She may even be nursing a guilty conscience because of it. So if her husband expresses how he experiences her unresponsiveness, it could be received with a general sense of relief. At least the subject is now on the 'marital agenda'. By using awareness exercises such as those outlined above, the subject can get out in the open where it can be dealt with more creatively and honestly. The old saying that 'a trouble shared is a trouble halved' has much truth in it in matters sexual.

Mutual coaching

Howard Clinebell points out an important role that lovers can play for one another:

> Discover what you enjoy most and coach each other on how to give maximum mutual enjoyment . . . do some explicit mutual coaching. Devote time to learning exactly how to make the other feel wonderful.[45]

Even the most accomplished lovers had to learn their techniques and knowledge of the opposite sex from someone else. Books can help, but you can't learn to swim merely from reading a book! Having a good sense of your own body is an advantage, but a good partner can bring out your own sense of value and affirm you in such a way that you can grow out of hang-ups quite quickly. As in other areas of an intimate life, regular affirmation and appreciation is a better stimulus to a satisfactory sex life than constant moaning and criticism. Don't expect your partner to get it right every time; the sad truth is that the earth is not going to move on every occasion you have sex together. For one thing, your moods will change. They will move across a wider range from a softly-softly experience of total gentleness and a slow pace to a hungry and urgent sexual gratification. In this matter you can coach your partner as to how he or she can help your arousal, stimulation, maintenance of erotic feelings and a satisfying orgasm.

Again and again, it is argued that people are too embarrassed to speak to one another explicitly where sex is concerned. Of course, it is possible for you to suffer in silence, but then you will always get the sex life you deserve! If speaking to your partner about your sexual preferences is hard, consider some of the following statements which may represent some of the things you would like to say to your partner, but never dared:

> 'Ooh, yes. Yes!'
> 'That's terrific!'
> 'Not so fast, darling!'
> 'Slow down a bit!'
> 'Harder!'
> 'You're hurting me!'

'Stroke me there!'
'Kiss me!'
'Hold me tighter!'
'Come inside!'
'Faster!'
'Let me come on top!'
'Yes, just there!'
'Oh, I love that!'
'That feels just perfect!'
'Don't stop!'
'You're fantastic!'

This kind of 'mutual coaching' is something anyone can learn once they take responsibility for the quality of their own sexual satisfaction. It's simply cheap – and wounding – to place the total responsibility for your sexual satisfaction upon your partner. It is copping-out on a grand scale, and it ruins thousands of marriages. It is up to *you* what you get out of sex – not to your partner. When I hear statements such as, 'He's hopeless in bed!' or, 'She just lays there; there's more life in a lettuce than in my wife!', much more is revealed about the complainer than their partner. I usually ask them, 'Why are you allowing your husband to be hopeless in bed?' or, 'Why do you let your wife just lie there like a lettuce?' Such probing questions often produce a denial, but behind this denial is either ignorance or avoidance. They either do not see that they are in any way responsible for 'coaching' their partner, or they simply avoid the responsibility by taking refuge in constant criticism – but never to their partner's face!

'Not tonight, darling!'

Life cannot always be perfect, and this truism certainly applies to sexual activity. There are going to be occasions when the 'Not-tonight-darling!' mode will be in operation. While there are going to be perfectly natural reasons for this, such as the 'time of the month' or tiredness, there are also other reasons that can lurk out of our awareness. I know of no better way of identifying such possible reasons than the following very helpful analysis by Sam Keen.[46]

If the husband just cannot get it up, or simply doesn't want to, he may be conveying one of the following important messages:

'No.'
'Not now.'
'I don't feel desire.'
'I am not ready to be intimate with you.'
'I don't know you well enough yet.'
'I'm afraid you will swallow me up, take all my time, energy and freedom.'
'I'm afraid I am not a good enough lover to satisfy you.'
'I'm afraid of the consequences.'
'I'm afraid to lose control.'
'I'm angry.'
'I don't want to give you pleasure.'
'I want to punish you for betraying me, ignoring me, using me, not taking me seriously.'
'I don't trust you.'
'I choose to withhold myself from you.'
'I resent your demands.'
'I am tired of pretending I am always powerful and in control.'
'Sometimes I am small and frightened and I want to be held.'
'I don't want to *do* anything.'
'I want you to make love to me.'
'I am tired of making it.'
'I want to lie back and be soft and let it happen.'
'I don't want to make love until I feel trust, tenderness and desire.'

While she, on the other hand, may be saying 'Not tonight darling!' because she feels:

'I am not moved.'
'I do not feel desire or love.'
'I do not want to be that vulnerable.'
'I am tired of being an object – a piece, a chick, a cunt, a wife, a thing.'
'If you do not want to engage my mind and my heart you cannot enter my body.'
'I'm not ready yet; take more time; touch me.'
'I want to be by and for myself now; independent.'
'I am free to be closed or open.'
'I don't want to be passive; I want to make love to you but my aggression frightens you.'
'I am afraid that if I lose control I will overwhelm you, or myself.'
'I feel guilty.'
'I have been hurt too much in the past and I am still afraid.'

No arbitrary lists like these can possibly be true for all of us all of the time. But I feel that Sam Keen has recognized with his characteristic perception and sensitivity what can often lie behind our 'not fancying it'. But it is only in the honesty and integrity of our own hearts that we can resolve the conflict between how we feel and what our partner expects of us. By listening to our body and attuning ourselves to its needs we learn to grow more whole. It is precisely that wholeness that we wish to share with our partner in order to enrich our shared experience of life.

Only through such depths of honesty (with ourselves as well as our partner) can the freedom and growth implicit in the ideas of the New Man and the New Woman emerge. Sam Keen concludes:

> The images we create recreate us. The old icons showed men and women as different species. Iron-hard men and flesh-soft women . . . Now a new image is emerging, a new ideal of the complete person. S/he has the capacity and the need to combine the opposites previously

> assigned to the separate sexes . . . The passage from the old ways is turbulent. Men often feel unmanly when they first abandon making, doing, and controlling and begin to feel warm and welcoming. It seems too passive to wait and wonder. Women are usually awkward when they first try to move with angular force . . . Beneath the confusion of sex roles . . . a new person is being born. It is time now for us to listen to our deepest desires and to learn from each other. Time for a new dialogue between power and love, the hard and soft ways of being in the world.[47]

These reflections pinpoint the issues we must face if we are to break out of constricting and harmful habits concerning our fulfilment as sexual beings. Sam Keen focuses on what a relationship between two totally open people, devoid of obsolete sexual stereotypes, could look like. It may appear to be utterly tantalizing but in my view it is possible to achieve this way of relating within the mutual care, trust and honesty of a stable, growing marriage.

Enriching your sexual intimacy, therefore, will mean giving serious thought to what attitudinal and behavioural changes you would like to see. It may involve having to face difficulties and embarrassments hidden for years. It will almost certainly mean the conscious abandonment of whatever legacy in your marriage of 'not saying' you discover in the process. If these changes can be accomplished within the safety of a mutual trust and commitment to one another's growth, then they are within reach and thoroughly worth investing energy in achieving. The Love-life Satisfaction Questionnaire is at least a starting point for you and your partner to explore these issues further.

13. Marriage Enrichment: The Outcome

Values of the process

There are many well-argued reasons in this book for the value of the process of marriage enrichment, and it may be helpful to summarize them at this point.

1. Marriage enrichment works best with stable, secure and basically sound marriages. It works on the principle of 'making good marriages better'. How are 'stable' and 'secure' to be assessed? No human relationship is problem-free – unless it is dead! It is a matter of balance. A 'good enough' marriage is one where, on the whole, things between the two people concerned are OK, and the income from the emotional investment in the marriage is basically satisfactory.
2. Marriage enrichment does not have to await the removal of all problems in the relationship; indeed, it can be a means to that end. On the analogy of human health, it is simply more efficient to keep a healthy body going, than to let it go to pot, and then get it repaired. Prevention is better than cure.
3. Marriage enrichment works at the prevention of serious break-down. Nothing is certain in human relationships and there is always the occasional ice-berg that any marriage can strike. However, when the relationship is such that it is worth preserving, the necessary energy can be found to do so.
4. The occasional reappraisal of a marriage can be like a

spring-clean of a house. We are surprised to discover things around the house once we start to move the furniture and look behind the curtains. Marriage enrichment is a means of spring-cleaning a marriage, seeing what needs throwing out or replacing.

5. Marriage enrichment focuses upon hidden assumptions and other blocks to growth in a marriage. It gives both partners the opportunity of realigning the marriage along contemporary needs rather than the out-dated ones which perhaps were relevant at the start of the relationship.
6. Physical check-ups are now common-place. They are a sign neither of a neurotic obsession with our health nor of a fear of illness. They are just plain common sense. Hence with marriage enrichment. There is nothing abnormal about checking up on our marriage, to feel its pulse, take its temperature and see what the blood-count looks like. Is it anaemic?
7. Marriage enrichment can help couples to look at what might happen if things go on as they are. It enables both partners to raise issues of common concern to the relationship and its general health. It assumes a common right to improve the relationship beyond its present generally satisfactory state.

On the principle that we usually reap what we sow, it would appear that most of us get the marriage we deserve.

Many couples who would consider their marriage stable and secure nevertheless may present many symptoms of a stale relationship. Marital ruts can become comfortable and secure, and neither partner may be prepared to shake its existing safe foundation. Perhaps some marriages considered 'sound' are in fact 'sound asleep'? What advantage could possibly accrue to such couples should they consider taking marriage enrichment seriously? Let's take Don and Doris as an example.

The story of Don and Doris

This couple have been married for twenty-four years, and the family have been making noises about their forthcoming silver wedding anniversary. As with most important anniversaries, this one has involved Don and Doris in some heart-searching about what they will be celebrating. Mere persistence? Force of habit? Inertia to change what they do not like? An ideal partnership?

Their marriage is certainly 'good enough' for both of them. They have learned to put up with the deficiencies of each other in the interests of not rocking the matrimonial boat. It would not be true to say that there are no apparent problems in Don's and Doris's marriage, nor is there any great joy. There is a rather boring regularity about the way they relate – well on the way to the Shirley Valentine scenario of egg and chips on Tuesdays, steak and chips on Thursdays! Don and Doris represent the kind of couple who work on the principle of 'least said soonest mended'. Each harbours resentment towards the other, but it never gets expressed openly. There are occasions when they resort to blaming and when understanding seems in short supply. Married life has become rather predictable, yet – to the outsider at least – it appears strong. Instead of 'settling up' in their marriage, through honest and loving confrontation, they have chosen to 'settle down' to a fairly conventional collusion. The name of this game is either 'Let's pretend!' or, more deviously, 'I won't say anything if you don't!'

As Don and Doris take their heads out of the daily routine and begin to look forward to the next twenty-five years of married life, several things come into focus. First, the children are now off their hands. The nest is now empty, apart from the occasional visits of children and the grandchildren. Next, both Don's and Doris's parents are approaching the time when decisions may have to be made concerning their future care. Will this fall upon Don and Doris? Can the family get together and think about what may be best for their ageing parents? Then there are the issues of forthcoming retirement and living off a pension. How will they manage financially? And do they need their five-bedroomed house now that the children are gone? Should they keep it on for the elderly parents to come and live with them? Or, should they move to a smaller house in the country? Big decisions await Don and Doris in the next few years.

But there are also big internal issues to be faced concerning the future of their relationship. As they face their own ageing process, what kinds of new needs now emerge? And do they have a flexible enough pattern of relating that allows for new ideas and fresh responses to these emerging situations?

Don and Doris noticed that their local parish church was arranging a marriage enrichment weekend at a conference centre in the country. The publicity looked fairly non-threatening and they already knew some couples who were planning to attend. They decided to join them. As the weekend drew nearer they began to have second thoughts but stuck to their original decision. At best, it probably couldn't do any harm.

The weekend arrived and they joined their friends on the coach that had been arranged to take them to the conference centre. Don and Doris had not attended anything like this before, so they felt very nervous. The first thing they noticed was how comfortable and welcoming the place was. More of a hotel, thought Doris. Refreshments were laid on for them on arrival, and they were asked to put name-tags on so that they could get to know one another. The party from their church numbered around a dozen, and there were some from other local churches who were strangers to them.

Once they had settled into their rooms, they had time to look round the bookstall and the gardens before dinner was served. At this point, Don and Doris noticed that the people seemed to keep very much to their local church groupings, but this pattern dissolved during the weekend into a more free-for-all gathering. After dinner, the first session took place in the large lounge. There were about thirty or so people, and Don noticed that their ages ranged from the mid-thirties to some in their sixties. The general feeling was one of nervousness and uncertainty about what they would have to do during the weekend. Doris wondered if all their matrimonial dirty linen would have to come out, while Don silently resolved to keep as quiet as possible.

Barry and Gwen, the leaders of the enrichment weekend, were obviously used to dealing with the Dons and Dorises of this world and immediately put most people at their ease. They spelt out some 'ground rules' for the weekend, which were as follows:

- It is OK to feel embarrassed/anxious/panicky.
- Be aware of what you are feeling – and own it.
- Be as real as you dare to be.
- You do not have to reveal anything that may embarrass either you or your partner.
- Take responsibility for what you choose to reveal and what you choose to withhold.
- The group will feel safer if everyone adheres to the usual assumption of confidentiality: you are not free to repeat outside this centre what others say.

The group was then asked to choose someone other than their partner and talk to them for about ten minutes about (a) what they feared most about the weekend; (b) what they hoped for from the weekend; (c) why they had come in the first place. Don found it easy to speak with Anne and he was surprised to find that she was as nervy as he was and, like him, resolved to say as little as possible.

They then came back into the larger group and some of them shared what they had said. Don was glad there was no pressure for him to speak openly but he felt comfortable about what he had shared with Anne. At the end of the session most of the members made for the bar; others to bed.

The next day it was like a holiday, especially for Doris, to come down and find breakfast ready – and no washing up. They managed to have a stroll in the lovely grounds before the first session. By this time, most of the early nerves had given way to a sense of expectancy.

The main session (with coffee in the middle) was spent working as couples on their own relationship. This made the session safer than in the larger group. Each couple was given some awareness exercises (such as, what it would feel like to be the other person), which they did individually and then checked out their performance with their partner. There were quite a few giggles during these exercises, and Don was glad to find that not everything was being taken too seriously. Fun was clearly included on the menu. Then they were asked to write a letter to their partner, being as honest as possible about how they felt their marriage could be enriched and including any changes they would like to see. They then read their letters to each other. This opened up quite a hornet's nest of unspoken resentments and grievances which had been simmering not too far beneath the surface of their marriage.

The leaders demonstrated a 'mirroring exercise' in which each partner spoke for two minutes without interruption. The other partner then had to repeat back as much as they could remember without prompting. Doris was clearly better at listening than Don, but they were asked to stick at it until most of what was being said was remembered and 'mirrored' back accurately. Don found that exercise hard work but very rewarding. Once they got the hang of really listening to one another, they were then asked to look at some of the issues raised in their letters and this led to a greater level of understanding of how each of them felt about their marriage and one another.

After lunch there was some free time to wander around the grounds or go into the local town. The leaders had offered counselling time for any couple who felt they would like to speak to the leaders in private, and some couples took advantage of this offer. After all, it was free.

After tea, there was time to work on the marital role expectation inventory, and Don and Doris found out a lot about each other as they worked their way through their individual expectations of one another. Don discovered that he would like to have more say in the decision-making process, more companionship from Doris and a greater awareness of his sexual needs. Doris discovered that she enjoyed her role as peace-maker to the family, hostess and involvement in the local church. She wished Don would join her in church activities and help more around the house. They were both surprised to find how easy it was to share these potential danger areas, as Don and Doris hardly ever dared to disagree with one another at home. Being with other couples who had come to work on their marriage somehow gave them permission to wander into these hitherto forbidden zones.

The main evening session was spent in the renegotiation process which was both introduced and illustrated through a role play by the leaders, Barry and Gwen. There was much laughter when Gwen played the part of a grumpy wife, and Barry took the part of the anxious husband who tried to appease her in every way he could. Most couples got the point, especially when a more positive way of relating was role-played. Don and Doris worked through the steps given to them by Barry and Gwen, noting areas of agreement – the strengths of their marriage – and agreeing to do some work on the areas that needed some renegotiating between them. This subject brought up other hidden areas that Don and Doris were not aware of, and both ended the day feeling that in spite of their twenty-four-year-old marriage, they were both beginning to understand themselves and one another much better. That night both felt closer to each other than for some time, and they found love-making both natural and fulfilling.

The final morning, after breakfast, Don and Doris were beginning to feel sad at the thought of returning home that evening, and were full of determination to make the most of the remaining time. During the conference, they had met many other couples, each battling with the problems of surviving the long-distance marriage. Clearly, some future friendships were in the making.

Barry and Gwen introduced the group to the idea of closing the 'escape hatches' in marriage. These represent all the artful ways people seek safety from their partners by 'escaping' activities. They usually drain energy away from the relationship by seeking to gratify their needs apart from their partner. Barry and Gwen did not advocate the 'Siamese twin' marriage whereby the couple do everything together, but invited couples to discover where their unhealthy escape hatches might be. They suggested some examples:

- Disappearing into the garage.
- Spending time at mother's.
- Volunteering for every committee at the church.
- Falling asleep on the couch.
- Working late at the office, etc.

The couples were then invited to complete the sentence, 'Starting this week, I agree to spend more time and energy in our relationship by . . .' (Here they could specify what action they intended in order to close the escape hatch.) They then shared what they had written with their partner. Doris felt a bit awkward when she added up all the hours she spent on church committees and the bit about escaping to the garage lay rather heavily on Don's conscience. They were honest enough to admit that sometimes they needed a break from one another, but in future they would admit this rather than take refuge in an excuse.

On the last day, they looked at the Enriching Marital Intimacy Check-list, and other bells were beginning to ring as they worked their way through the list of twelve potential strata of intimacy. Some of the items they would never have thought of as having anything to do with intimacy, but the introduction Barry and Gwen gave to the check-list made them think otherwise. Don remarked to Doris how easy it seemed to learn in this environment, since no one was telling them how to run their marriage or doling out good advice. They were clearly being treated as adults, capable of making sensible decisions for their own marriage. No one's dirty linen was washed in public, and privacy was respected.

That evening, they took part in a group farewell, which focused upon a celebration of the Holy Communion service in the conference chapel. Don thought he would feel 'out of it', but the friendly atmosphere and the non-threatening leadership made him relax enough to enjoy it. The chaplain prayed for each couple as they came to the communion table, and Don and Doris felt it was like reaffirming their marriage vows. It was a moment of rare emotion for them both, and there were some tears as people left the chapel. Don felt his were tears of joy and gratitude for Doris's companionship, and he clasped her hand lovingly.

Of course, no single illustration could do justice to the complexity of needs at a marriage enrichment weekend. Asked what the weekend had meant to them, I think Don and Doris would say that it had opened up their channels of communication once more. The weekend also opened some windows in the relationship and let fresh air waft through what was, on their own admission, getting a rather stale marriage. They learned to talk to one another, and to listen to one another, not in order to blame for what was wrong in the marriage but in order to discover how, together, they could work towards putting things right. The weekend meant that they now had a practical agenda to work on, and had found some communication skills with which to do this.

Thousands of couples have reason to be grateful for such an opportunity as these weekends afford – and thousands more would do so if only they knew about them. While, for most couples, the best course would be to attend such a weekend, if this is not practicable much may be gained by reading this book with your partner and doing the exercises, in order to raise your awareness of ways to improve the potential of your partnership. Since no marriage is ever perfect, there is always room for improvement.

The clue to such improvements is certainly based on an ability to listen and respond to our partners. 'Not listening' is the biggest source of complaint in marital counselling, and naturally so. For if we are neither speaking nor listening to our partner we cannot truly know them, and that impedes the intimacy necessary for our mutual growth and enjoyment. Good intentions are never enough; there needs to be practical implementation of those good intentions if we are to have the strong and rewarding marriages that most of us need.

A final word

My hope is that this book may act as a sign-post for you, wherever your marriage is at this point. You may be strolling along the marital path, or thinking about a detour, or simply feeling you have hit a No Through Road. Wherever you are in your marriage you certainly don't have to remain stuck. The potential for growth is always present, providing both of you are willing to put some energy into improving your relationship. If you are not happy with your marriage the way it is, you can say so. I hope I have suggested some ways in which you can do this and so find greater fulfilment in the love and acceptance that is waiting to be discovered in your marriage.

Postscript: 'I still choose you again . . .'

I was deeply moved when I first read these words from a book by an American clergyman.[48] They are addressed by Charles L. Rassieur to his wife, Ginni, and represent for me the essence of a growing marriage contract based on a conscious renewal of their commitment in spite of (or because of) the pressures to which they are subject in their work. They model an open and honest expression of love.

I'm glad, Ginni, that not many years ago we agreed that our marriage would be based on our continuing to rechoose each other. In effect, we decided our marriage would not be a life sentence, but a commitment intentionally reaffirmed each day. More importantly, that means that I am living with you because I really want to. We also know that that decision is faced by both of us in the numerous relationships we have with others outside our marriage. When you are with other men and I am with other women, we must deal with a continuing choice whether we still want to live with each other. You are still an essential part of my life, and that's why today I choose you again as the one with whom I want to share my life.

I suppose to be honest I have to say that some of the feelings I have occasionally had toward a few counsellees did cause me to wonder if I wanted to continue renewing our contract. But I must add that till now no other woman has really made me look at that too seriously. None the less, there have been times of searching in my heart – as probably you too have reflected deeply about your own continuing choice of me.

Today I choose you again for my wife for some reasons that are particularly important to me – reasons that have a lifelong quality. It is important to me that you are an open and growing person. You surely aren't the same person I married! Sometimes I like that and sometimes I don't. We've talked about that, haven't we? But more often than not I like the way you have a firmer grasp on who you are and what you want.

That means you are clearly distinct from me. There isn't that old dependence on me that I think got burdensome for both of us despite how we both thought we liked it. But best of all I like your strength. You aren't made of eggshells. You are able to take care of your own feelings, and knowing that, I feel more comfortable about sharing with you the parts of me I'm more sensitive about.

I choose you again today because you are honest with me. You're honest about your feeling angry and hurt. And when I've lost my perspective on a counsellee you were affected, your honest feedback was what I needed.

I choose you again because you're sexy. You really like your sexuality, more so, I think you would agree, in the last several years. I experience you as being open now not only to your sexual side but also to what it means for me as a man – especially as your husband – to be sexual. Sure, some other women look pretty interesting to me sometimes, but I honestly doubt that they could be any more fun.

And I still choose you because you trust me. No doubt I have to cultivate some of that trust in responsible ways. But you affirm my own innate sense of freedom by your trust, and it is vital for me to claim my own freedom even when I am relating to other women. I choose you because I can trust you too, as you express and live out your freedom. Trust and freedom, they have to go together for us, don't they?

Finally, I choose you because I can't think of anyone else with whom I would rather face the future. The future is so uncertain sometimes. Our feelings are often unpredictable. It's scary to me when I realize we are both changing. What if you stopped choosing me but I still wanted you? I hate to think about that possibility. That's why a part of me wants to control you absolutely so you will always stay just as you are right now. Never change. But how dull! I think that would soon be utterly boring. So go ahead, change. I really want that risk for you and I want it for me.

I choose you again today for the coming years because in our individual freedom I feel we have fashioned a profound commitment to each other, and that gives me a confident feeling about you and about me. It's a confidence that somehow we will deal with the threats that most surely will come to our marriage. It's a confidence that helps me know that I will be able to deal with myself in the close and sometimes intense relationships I will have with others I am trying to help.

I choose you again now because you are really you, and I am I, and the commitment bound up in our individual freedom has become so essential to my being that I had to choose you today, just as now I expect to make the same choice again tomorrow.

Appendix A: Enriching Second Marriages

Some problems and possibilities of the second time around

According to a report from the Central Statistical Office, the number of marriages in which at least one of the partners was divorced rose from 34,000 in 1961 to 132,000 in 1988. Allowing for the partners from the same broken marriage subsequently remarrying, this still amounts to around a quarter of a million people entering second marriages each year. The research findings concerning second marriages is that they are far more at risk than first marriages.[49]

Many people reading this are likely to be in their second marriage. There is nothing in this book that will not apply to such marriages, but there are special factors that need mentioning.

The problem of bad endings

Some marriages end on a note of optimism. When two people can no longer live together in mutual trust, love and harmony it may be that separation and an amicable divorce is considered by both partners to be a desirable option. This sometimes happens in an atmosphere free of recriminations and blame, and even in a spirit of harmony and friendship.

But while amicable endings do exist, they are probably in the minority. Bitterness, anger, accusation and counter-accusation, hurt and pain are the experience of many people whose marriages end in separation. When they have left their partner, or been left by them, there remains a wound which sometimes seems will never heal. The pain is often all-consuming. Feelings of worthlessness, failure, betrayal and resentment seem to go on forever. We find ourselves unforgiving of our partner and unforgiving of ourselves.

Life itself often seems futile. There appears to be no future and we feel trapped in the legacy of the past. Such painful endings have two major effects upon people. First, they can make people feel the kind of things I have just been describing above, and this lowers their self-esteem and sense of value. Secondly, it either makes them vow never to get involved again in any serious relationship or, paradoxically, it makes them throw themselves headlong into a new relationship in order to forget the pain of ending the previous one. For such people, Boswell's *Life of Samuel Johnson*, contains a phrase that may not be without relevance: 'A gentleman who had been very unhappy in marriage, married immediately after his wife died: Johnson said, "It was the triumph of hope over experience." '

This paradox comprises a choice between (a) *self-imposed isolation*, with its total loss of trust in others and in our own ability to form and maintain meaningful relationships, and (b) *self-forgetfulness* by absorption into another relationship. Both involve massive denial. By *self-imposed isolation* we deny our own essential goodness and our abilities to form loving relationships; by *self-forgetfulness* we deny the pain we are feeling and, however unconsciously, place upon another person the responsibility for making us feel happy again. Long-term relationships based on such denial are usually flawed from the outset. Bad endings usually result in bad beginnings, especially when there are resident ghosts!

The ghosts of the past

The majority, if not all, of failed marriages contain several ghosts, and it is important for the future happiness of those who are separated or divorced to be aware of them and deal with them creatively.

Such ghosts include:

- the characteristics of the previous partner;
- the 'game plan' for the former marriage;
- the expectations of both ourselves and our former spouse;
- the unmet needs in the failed marriage;
- the pain of the past.

These are just a few possibilities by way of illustrating what 'marital ghosts' are and their effect on second marriages unless there is a conscious attempt to exorcize them.

It is a source of never-failing amazement how some people seem to choose second partners who are identikit 'look-alikes' to their former wife or husband. I recall one woman who had spent many unhappy years trying (unsuccessfully) to come to terms with her uncaring husband who used to beat her up regularly. Finally, after much heart-searching, she found the courage to separate from him, but within a short while she was married to another man who had all the characteristics of her former husband. It seems against all reason, but such stories are more commonplace than you may imagine. The intricacies behind such seemingly flawed choices would better be served by a period in therapy in order to discover what was going on underneath the surface of this woman's consciousness. One man, who made similar choices in his relationships, told me that he seemed pre-destined to choose female partners who were 'short, dark, and determined'. I asked him who this description fitted, and he muttered, sheepishly, 'My mother!' There are ghosts in the lives of such people, and until they are identified and dealt with creatively they will go on interfering with their happiness.

The 'game plan' of a previous marriage also needs to be understood, if we are to recognize and revise the rocks on which our previous marriage foundered. For instance, in marriages where there is a very definite 'One up, one down' relationship, we may seek out another partner who will play this game with us, no matter whether we were the 'up' partner or the 'down' one. (Perhaps this is what the woman referred to above was doing, unconsciously seeking out another man who would keep her in the down position.) If the previous marriage was one of those I call a 'Peter Pan and Wendy' marriage, it is almost certain that the Peter Pans of this world will seek out another Wendy, and *vice versa*. If the former marriage was a 'Siamese twin' marriage, where there was no individual identity but a corporate one, glued to the other partner, then it is likely that a future partner will be sought who has a better kind of 'super glue' than the previous partner. Rather than perform their own inner post-mortem of the death of the former marriage, many people unthinkingly rush into another relationship having learned nothing from the mistakes of the past. (For a fuller treatment of these and other unhealthy models of relationships see my *Couples in Counselling*, chapter 9.)

The expectations that each partner had in the first marriage also need to be consciously checked out. How realistic were they in the first place? Did a former wife expect her husband to be perfect, and he failed her? How far did each of them try to meet the other's expectations for perfection before they inevitably failed? Did a former husband expect his wife to be the ideal housekeeper, hostess, mother, sex partner, cook? Such husbands – and their former wives – need to revise such unrealistic expectations before they place them upon another unsuspecting victim who, like the previous wife, is also bound to fail. Husbands who were expected to be perfect time-keepers, high-flying achievers to keep their wives in the manner of life to which they had become accustomed, or ideal fathers to their children, need to take a step back from such expectations to find out for themselves how far they were realistic.

Unmet needs also form a large area that can create enormous dissatisfaction in second marriages. Unrecognized, they can form a very large and voracious 'ghost'. We can unconsciously seek out a future partner who will meet all the needs our former partner manifestly failed to meet. Some of our needs, of course, are entirely unrealistic and, in fact, could be dated back to our childhood. While forming part of a natural expectation of a child – that he or she should be supplied with adequate physical and emotional resources, appropriate to their status as a child – these needs become totally inappropriate when transferred to an adult relationship. Many marriages, while appearing to be adult choices on a conscious level, are in fact a veiled attempt to recreate the circumstances of childhood. A man chooses a wife, but really needs a mother; a woman chooses a husband, but really needs a father. Of course, such unrealistic (and hidden) needs often prove a fatal obstacle when brought into a contemporary marriage.

Our very pain at the ending of a previous marriage can also form another important 'ghost' in any subsequent union. We may need future partners to heal the hurt our past husbands or wife inflicted upon us. We need not so much a partner as a nurse!

Thus, when we come to the enrichment of a second or subsequent marriage, we should bear in mind some of the implications and circumstances of our former relationship, and have some clear ideas as to where, and why, it went wrong. These thoughts should be shared frankly and openly with our future partner so that they can be aware of our 'ghosts' and how their help and energy can be enlisted to ensure that these ghosts do not insiduously enter the new relationship to haunt it.

Second marriages do not necessarily have to be viewed, as Dr Johnson saw it, as a 'triumph of hope over experience'. Having made, and learned from, our mistakes in the past, we are able to bring a greater wisdom and a more realistic vision into our second marriage.

Note. I intend making the important subject of how to make leavetaking a creative experience the subject of a fourth, and final, volume in this series.

Appendix B: Some Useful Addresses

Association for Marriage Enrichment
c/o Westminster Pastoral Foundation
23 Kensington Square
London W8 5HN
Tel. 071 937 6956

Family Life and Marriage Education (FLAME)
c/o C. of E. Board for Social Responsibility
Church House
Great Smith Street
London SW1P 3NZ

Anglican Marriage Encounter
Derrick and Jen Gierth
5 Holme Road
Bingham
Nottingham NG13 8DZ
Tel. 0949 37519

Catholic Marriage Encounter
Bob and Flora Bell
6 Cotton Field Road
Withington
Manchester M20 9QW
Tel. 061 434 7303

Baptist Marriage Encounter
Bill and Brenda Reynolds
26 Bellingdon Road
Chesham
Bucks HP5 2HA
Tel. 0494 782466

Mission to Marriage
Dave and Joyce Ames
20 Mill Street
Mildenhall
Suffolk IP28 7DP
Tel. 0638 713047

The Cherwell Centre
14 Norham Gardens
Oxford
Tel. 0865 52106
(run occasional marriage growth and enrichment weekends)

Worldwide Marriage Encounter (Catholic)
John and Maria Price
110 Lightwoods Road
Bearwood
Warley
West Midlands B67 5BH
Tel. 021 420 1148

Marriage Alive (Christian Weekend Course)
Richard Conner
Pinmill
Cherry Garden Lane
Danbury
Essex CM3 4QP
Tel. 024541 2448

Notes

1. Office of Population Censuses and Surveys, *Marriage and Divorce Statistics 1937–1983* (HMSO 1990).
2. Sam Keen, *The Passionate Life* (Gateway Books 1985), p. 104
3. David Cooper, *The Death of the Family* (Penguin 1971), pp. 24–8.
4. Khoren Arisian, *The New Wedding* (Vintage Books 1973), p. 3.
5. Madonna Kolbenschlag, *Kiss Sleeping Beauty Good-bye* (Harper & Row 1988), p. 122.
6. *The Times*, 3 February 1988.
7. Office of Population Censuses and Surveys, *OPCS Monitor: General Household Survey, Preliminary Results for 1983* (HMSO).
8. OPCS, op. cit.
9. *The Daily Telegraph*, 11 June 1990.
10. Christopher Clulow, *Marital Therapy* (Aberdeen University Press 1985), p. 5.
11. Anne Dickson, *A Woman in Your Own Right* (Quartet Books 1982).
12. OPCS, *Marriage and Divorce Statistics.*
13. Betty Yorburg, *The Changing Family* (Columbia University Press 1973), p. 12.
14. Nena and George O'Neill, *Open Marriage* (Avon 1972), p. 40.
15. M. Scott Peck, *The Road Less Travelled* (Touchstone 1978), p. 98.
16. Will Schutz, *Profound Simplicity* (Turnstone Books 1979), p. 82.
17. Peter McWilliams, from *Come Love with Me and Be My Life* (Leo Press, Michigan, 1971).
18. Jeni Couzyn, *House of Changes* (Heinemann 1978).
19. Schutz, op. cit., pp. 3–4.
20. Betty Friedan, *The Feminine Mystique* (Penguin 1963).
21. Elaine Storkey, *What's Right with Feminism?* (SPCK 1985), p. 67.
22. Germaine Greer, *The Female Eunuch* (MacGibbon & Kee 1970).
23. Harold I. Lief in his foreword to Larry Hof and William R. Miller, *Marriage Enrichment* (Robert J. Brady Co. 1981).

24. Harville Hendrix, *Getting the Love You Want* (Harper & Row 1989), p. xvii.
25. Tony Gough, *Couples in Counselling* (Darton Longman & Todd 1989), chapter 9.
26. Larry Hof and William R. Miller, *Marriage Enrichment* (Robert J. Brady Co. 1981), pp. 8–9.
27. Shirley G. Luthman and Martin Kirschenbaum, *The Dynamic Family* (Palo Alto 1974).
28. *The Daily Telegraph*, 13 June 1990.
29. Sam Keen, *To a Dancing God* (Fontana 1970), p. 116.
30. Harville Hendrix, op. cit., p. xiv.
31. *The Daily Telegraph*, 11 June 1990.
32. Polly Toynbee, writing in *The Guardian*, 6 April 1987.
33. Hof and Miller, op. cit., p. 111.
34. Tony Gough, *Couples Arguing* (Darton Longman & Todd 1987).
35. Tom Oden, *Game Free: the Meaning of Intimacy* (Harper & Row 1974), p. 31.
36. Oden, op. cit., p. 3f.
37. Howard J. Clinebell and Charlotte H. Clinebell, *The Intimate Marriage* (Harper & Row 1970), p. 37f.
38. Howard J. Clinebell, *Growth Counselling for Marriage Enrichment* (Fortress Press 1975), p. 18.
39. John C. Haskey, 'Grounds for Divorce in England and Wales – A Social and Demographic Analysis', *Journal of Biosocial Science* (vol. 18, 1986), p. 139.
40. Robin Skynner, in *The Weekend Guardian*, 10 February 1990.
41. John Powell, *Why Am I Afraid to Tell You Who I Am?* (Fontana 1975).
42. Sheldon Kopp, *Who Am I . . . Really?* (Jeremy P. Tarcher 1987), p. 210f.
43. Erich Fromm, *The Art of Loving* (Unwin Books 1975), p. 48.
44. Fromm, op. cit., p. 11.
45. Howard J. Clinebell, *Growth Counselling for Mid-Years Couples* (Fortress Press 1977), p. 55.
46. Sam Keen, *The Passionate Life* (Gateway Books 1985), pp. 154–5.
47. Ibid., p. 155.
48. Charles L. Rassieur, *The Problem Clergymen Don't Talk About* (Westminster John Knox 1976), pp. 150–2.
49. Central Statistical Office, *Social Trends 20* (HMSO 1990).

Further Reading

Second Honeymoon, Dave and Joyce Ames (Kingsway Publications, 1989)
Getting The Love You Want, Harville Hendrix (Harper & Row, NY, 1988)
The Intimate Marriage, Howard J. Clinebell and Charlotte H. Clinebell (Harper & Row, NY, 1970)
Growth Counselling for Marriage Enrichment, Howard J. Clinebell (Fortress Press, Pa, 1975)
Growth Counselling for Mid-Years Couples, Howard J. Clinebell (Fortress Press, Pa, 1977)
Couples Arguing: Guidelines to Effective Communication, Tony Gough (Darton, Longman & Todd, 1987)
Couples in Counselling: A Consumer's Guide to Marriage Counselling, Tony Gough (Darton, Longman & Todd, 1989)
Don't Blame Me!: How to Stop Blaming Yourself and Other People, Tony Gough (Sheldon Press, 1990)

Index